Time to Love
Time for War
Time to Heal

DAVID BEBELAAR

Time

Tellwell Talent
www.tellwell.ca

ISBN
978-0-2288-0732-2 (Hardcover)
978-0-2288-0611-0 (Paperback)

Dedication

"I would like to dedicate *Time*, *Time* to Love *Time* for War *Time* to Heal to the memory of my Opa, Oma and Father. Finding your letters was a gift. A gift that has allowed me to honor your Passion, your Honesty, your Compassion and your Morale guidance. The dedication to family that sustained you through the absolute worst of times was a Legacy that you passed down to my father, which I am so thankful for. Your Legacy does not end, we continue to Honor you with our dedication to family."

Table of Contents

Bäbler

Foreword

Throughout my life, I have experienced the effects of a war my father endured as a young boy. Having lived in a concentration camp as a child and having never really known his own father, who was also a victim of war, my father was inflicted with a wound so deep, it never did heal. He was never able to come to peace with all that had happened.

After my father's passing, I began to wonder where we, as a family, came from. I knew the geographical area and the family lineage, as we have an in-depth family tree, but what was more important to me was knowing what my grandparents had been like. As my father had no recollection of his father, I had no idea about my grandfather's character. Also, my grandmother passed away when I was only three years old, so I wondered what she had been like, too.

To my surprise, countless letters and correspondence, written to and from family members before and immediately after WWII, had been safely tucked away by my Oma and ultimately my father. I discovered them after my father passed away. My father had the capacity to read these letters, as most were written in Dutch, but the emotions they brought forward, he could not endure. He had tried to read selected items but could not get past the first couple of pages. I had not been made aware of these items prior to his passing.

Knowing where we have come from is an essential part of any family. The Bebelaar family has a well-documented family genealogy dating back to 1538, in the canton of Glarus, Switzerland, under the name Babler. (The name change, from Babler to Bebelaar, came about in 1811.) The family history is well documented, with names and dates, but it does not capture the essence of the individuals. The collective memory of the individuals is passed down through the generations, but when generations undergo horrific circumstances, that continuity is lost. The following compilation of letters and other correspondence creates a profile of the grandparents I never knew, as constructed through their own words, and the words of others who were close to them. It is a collective memory established through the writings of individuals who unfortunately were not able to pass their information directly down to the next generations.

Introduction

David Bebelaar was born December 20, 1886 in Rotterdam, Netherlands. On June 8, 1910, he married Aagje Anneke Visser, who was born June 14, 1882, in the nearby town of Kralingen a former village, now a neighbourhood of Rotterdam, located 3km east of the city. David worked as an accountant. Aagje worked as a seamstress. They were my paternal great-grandparents, and together they had five boys:

Jacob (my grandfather), also known as Jaap, born May 9, 1911
Nicolaas, also known as Nico, born July 2, 1912
Dirk, born October 13, 1913
Addriaan, also known as Aat, born September 4, 1918
David, born May 31, 1921

David Bebelaar was very proud to become a father when Jacob was born in May 1911. He named his son after his own father, Jacob, who was born on May 9, 1855. To commemorate the occasion of the birth of his grandson, Jacob presented to David, a pocket watch, inscribed JAC B, D z. Dz represents Davids zon (son).

This happy family was thriving when, on January 14, 1930, they lost Aagje. She had been stricken with goiter and passed away at the age of 48. The following year, on August 12, 1931, David Bebelaar remarried. His housekeeper, Leonora Wilhemina van der Voort, became his new wife, and together they brought an additional four children into the Bebelaar home:

Gerrit, also known as Gary, born October 12, 1932
Hans, born June 28, 1941

Jacob, also known as Jaap, born February 25, 1945
Leonora Agatha, born September 20, 1946

This large intergenerational family is where this story starts. Specifically, it follows the path of David and Aagje Bebelaar's eldest son, Jacob (my grandfather), born in 1911.

Jacob (Jaap) Bebelaar

David and Aagje Bebelaar with their first two children: Jacob and Nico.

Jacob (Jaap) Bebelaar, born May 9, 1911, is three years old at the outset of World War 1 (1914-1918). The Netherlands takes a neutral position during the First World War but is not immune to all of its ramifications. The Dutch economy is devastated by military blockades, and the population endures levels of starvation, as the import of food items is vastly limited. In the post-WWI period, it is normal for able-bodied men to be conscripted into military service when they reach the age of 19. This is the case for Jaap. He achieves a high school education, and on December 8, 1930 Jaap enters the Dutch military reserves in the 15th Infantry Regiment. His abilities are deemed less appropriate for naval duties, as he has previously had a hernia and is shortsighted, requiring glasses.

Jaap is quickly promoted to the rank of corporal in April of 1931, and by September 1931 he reaches the rank of sergeant. At this time, he is given a leave.

Jaap, by all accounts, is the typical dutiful oldest child. He studies accounting and becomes an assistant accountant, following in his father's footsteps. Jaap works with his father in the family accounting firm, but he also has another passion, music. Jaap is an accomplished violinist and he teaches violin at the Odd Fellows Youth Club in Rotterdam.

Jaap playing his violin, while brother Nico teases him by plugging his ears.

Plugging one's ears is not the norm when Jaap performs. On January 14, 1933, Jaap performs at the Odd Fellows Youth Club, as violinist, in four pieces: "Wild Rose" by R. Eulenberg, "Ave Verum" by W.A. Mozart, "Romance" by Joh. Svendsen and "Meditation De Thais" by J. Massenet. These four pieces are performed with a soprano, a violinist and a pianist.

Jaap's passion for music quickly turns to romance. He meets a wonderful young lady, a soprano who sings with him during the performance at the Odd Fellows Youth club. This accomplished young singer, Andrea (Bé) Oltmans, soon becomes the love of his life.

Andrea Pieternella Johanna Oltmans

Andrea Pieternella Johanna Oltmans is born in Apeldoorn, Netherlands on October 21, 1911 to parents Jan Jacob Oltmans and Alegonda Oltmans-Bemond. Andrea is the youngest of three girls, and is forever nicknamed Bé, for baby of the family. Her two older sisters were named Kor and Nel.

Jan Jacob Oltmans and Alegonda Oltmans-Bemond,
12 ½ wedding anniversary, December 1917

Andrea (Bé) Oltmans

Andrea is an accomplished singer. Her soprano voice is showcased in a performance on April 27, 1931 where she has a solo performance of three songs. She continues to perform and meets Jaap prior to their performance together in January 1933.

For Andrea music is a passion, but also a hobby. She enrolls in school to become a pharmacy assistant, and, on May 10, 1933, she passes her examinations to accomplish this goal. She finds employment working for a pharmacist, D. van Dijk, in Hillegersberg, a suburb or Rotterdam. She works there until October 1936.

The 1930s: A Decade of Crisis, Happiness and Success

Globally, the 1930s is the decade of the Great Depression. After the stock market crash in the United States in 1929, the economic crisis is rampant around the world. The depression in the Netherlands is primarily associated with the economics of European countries, mostly Germany, after World War I. The Netherlands feel the biggest impact of the depression between the years 1933 and 1936.

Jaap Bebelaar works with his father, David Bebelaar, and brother, Nico Bebelaar, at the family accounting firm. The Netherlands' economic crisis has a large effect on the family business, making it difficult to keep the business alive during this period.

1930

In 1930, Jaap and Bé both turn 19 and are looking forward to the years ahead. Bé enrolls in the Rijks University, School of Pharmacy to study to become a pharmacy assistant. The university is located in Utrecht. December 8 of 1930, Jaap enters the Dutch military for his compulsory service. He is assigned to the infantry.

1931 Bebelaar, Jacob

Geboren op 9 Mei 1911 te Rotterdam

Vader David

Moeder Visser, Aagje Anneke

Ingelijfd (l. p.) (b. t.) op 8 December 1930 als G. D. van de lichting 1931

uit Rotterdam, lot.nr. [illegible]

bij [illegible] Regiment infanterie [illegible]

[illegible]

5 Sept.	19 31	groot verlof.
5 Sept.	19 [illegible]	terug.
20 Sept.	19 [illegible]	groot verlof.
	19	terug.
	19	groot verlof.
	19	terug.
	19	groot verlof.

M. I. v. 19 ontslagen wegens

11646 - '40

1931

In 1931, Bé and Jaap are both experiencing the successes that young people do as they grow as adults. On April 2, 1931, Jaap is promoted to the rank of corporal, after only four months in the military. Later the same month, April 27, 1931, Bé and her soprano voice are showcased in a performance for the Association of "Old" Groningers: former residents of Groningen, a City in the northern Netherlands. This is the musical group's silver jubilee (25 years). Bé's performance is the 7th of the evening, and she performs three songs. She is also heavily involved with her studies during this time period.

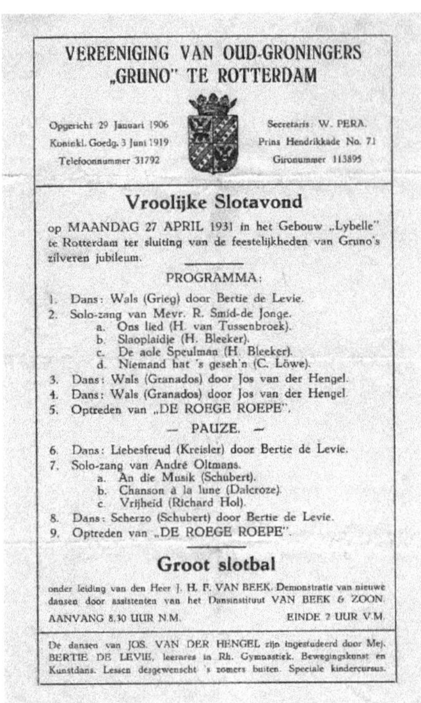

VEREENIGING VAN OUD-GRONINGERS
„GRUNO" TE ROTTERDAM

Opgericht 29 Januari 1906
Koninkl. Goedg. 3 Juni 1919
Telefoonnummer 31792

Secretaris: W. PERA.
Prins Hendrikkade No. 71
Gironummer 113895

Vroolijke Slotavond

op MAANDAG 27 APRIL 1931 in het Gebouw „Lybelle" te Rotterdam ter sluiting van de feestelijkheden van Gruno's zilveren jubileum.

PROGRAMMA:

1. Dans: Wals (Grieg) door Bertie de Levie.
2. Solo-zang van Mevr. R. Smid-de Jonge.
   a. Ons lied (H. van Tussenbroek).
   b. Slaoplaidje (H. Bleeker).
   c. De aole Speulman (H. Bleeker).
   d. Niemand hat 's geseh'n (C. Löwe).
3. Dans: Wals (Granados) door Jos van der Hengel.
4. Dans: Wals (Granados) door Jos van der Hengel.
5. Optreden van „DE ROEGE ROEPE".

— PAUZE. —

6. Dans: Liebesfreud (Kreisler) door Bertie de Levie.
7. Solo-zang van André Oltmans.
   a. An die Musik (Schubert).
   b. Chanson à la lune (Dalcroze).
   c. Vrijheid (Richard Hol).
8. Dans: Scherzo (Schubert) door Bertie de Levie.
9. Optreden van „DE ROEGE ROEPE".

Groot slotbal

onder leiding van den Heer J. H. F. VAN BEEK. Demonstratie van nieuwe dansen door assistenten van het Dansinstituut VAN BEEK & ZOON.

AANVANG 8.30 UUR N.M. EINDE 2 UUR V.M.

De dansen van JOS. VAN DER HENGEL zijn ingestudeerd door Mej. BERTIE DE LEVIE, leerares in Rh. Gymnastiek, Bewegingskunst en Kunstdans. Lessen desgewenscht 's zomers buiten. Speciale kindercursus.

On September 6, 1931, Jaap is once again recognized for his leadership, earning a promotion to the rank of sergeant. As his reserve platoon is finished its military exercises, he is allowed to go on leave.

Jaap in his military uniform with sergeant stripes

1932

1932 is the year that changes the lives of both Bé and Jaap. Jaap is embracing life. He meets the love of his life at a Sinterklaas party in December 1932. Jaap and Bé become a couple very quickly. He feels they are an ideal couple.

1933

On January 14, 1933 Jaap and Bé perform together at the Odd Fellow Youth Club. Performance 2b is a performance of "Ave Verum" featuring Bé, Jaap and a pianist. Jaap is very involved with the Youth Club, teaching violin to the youth. He is the violin player in all the performances this night, as well as acting in the play as the fifth performance, which also includes his younger brother Nico.

= PROGRAMMA =

1. OPENING
2. a. WILDE ROSE . . . R. Eulenburg (zang - piano)
   b. AVE VERUM . . W. A. Mozart (zang - viool - piano)
   c. ROMANCE . . . . Joh. Svendsen (viool - piano)
   d. MÉDITATION DE THAÏS J. Massenet (viool - piano)
   sopraan . Bé Oltmans   viool . Jaap Bebelaar   piano . Franz Andersen
3. LEVENSLIEDJES . . . . Daan Hooykaas
4. a. ROSAMUNDE . . Fr. v. Schubert   b. BEIERSCHE FANTASIE
   Plastische dansen, uitgevoerd door de dames Fieke Roosch & Mimi van Alphen.
5. EEN REUZE IDEÉ . BLIJSPEL IN 2 BEDRIJVEN VAN WILLY CORSARI.
   Regie: Dhr. S. Schaap

Personen:
Mevr. VERMEULEN . Dicky v. d. Graaff
FRITS, haar zoon . . . . Daan Hooykaas
KITTY, haar dochter . . . . Jo van Gils
ANNIE, haar dienstbode . . Bep de Graaf
FRANK, haar zwager . . . . Piet Roosch
Mevr. VAN DALEN . . . . Annie Haan
BLOM . . . . Jaap Bebelaar
vader van Mevr. Vermeulen
PIMP . . . . Nico Bebelaar

PAUZE tusschen het eerste en tweede bedrijf.

6. SLUITING.

Conferencier:
Dhr. D. HOOYKAAS

= BAL =

Muzikale medewerking van „THE SMITH' PLAYERS"

Vleugel geleverd door Firma C. Quispel

Bé successfully completes her courses at the university, and, on May 10, 1933, she passes her examinations and becomes a pharmacy assistant. She finds work in a pharmacy run by D. Van Dijk, in Hillegersberg, near Rotterdam.

1934

October 21, 1934 marks the next milestone in their relationship: the engagement announcement. The date coincides with Bé's 23rd birthday.

VERLOOFD:

ANDRÉ OLTMANS
EN
J. BEBELAAR

ROTTERDAM, 21 OCTOBER 1934
ROCHUSSENSTRAAT 327 B
BEUKELSWEG 94 D

GEEN RECEPTIE

The letters of congratulations start to flow in. Based on the first letter, it is apparent the family had advance knowledge that this engagement was to occur.

Groede, 19 October 1934

Dear Bé and Jaap,

Congratulations on your engagement, and I hope that you two will be very happy. And Bé, congratulations on your birthday. This is an extraordinary day for you, Bé. I hope that you, my youngest sister, always look back on this day with happiness.

Here is a present from Bram and me. It is something extravagant, but now that we can get it for the first time, I allowed myself to get it for you. In the future I will buy you practical things.

It would be so nice if I could be with you this day. In my thoughts, I will be with you the whole day.

Bé, write me a long letter next week.

Bye, bye. Many greetings for both of you, and a kiss for Bé.

From NEL

After the engagement is announced, stories start to come out about the two of them. Some of the stories are alluded to in the next letter. They are young lovers, and, as their grandson, it warms my heart to hear of their connection.

Rotterdam, 20 - 10 - 1934

Dear Bé and Jaap,

First of all, congratulations on your engagement.

We better not tell about the first steps on the road that lead to this first milestone.

We vaguely remember camping out with Jaap, who was dressed in a dirty polo shirt with washed-out colours and an amorous look in his eyes. Bé dressed slightly better but with the same look in her eyes, and we remember more of these symptoms, that would lead to a sure engagement.

We won't say more, because you can rightly say, "The pot and kettle are tarred with the same brush." Maybe there will be an occasion when you two can tell similar things about us.

We also hope that the first steps will lead to many more milestones as real globetrotters and the hope of a long and happy life—who knows, may be 100 years.

Bé and Jaap, we, your "rivals," sincerely hope there is a good, happy future in store for you.

From Jo & Dick

PS Also, our congatulations to your parents and families. Jo.

1935

By 1935, the depression has taken hold of the Dutch economy and the family accounting firm is struggling. The brothers in the firm, Jaap and Nico, start to look for other opportunities. They are each looking to start their adult lives, and for Jaap, a newly engaged man, he is wanting to provide for his bride-to-be.

1936

In early 1936, the search for work continues. Jaap applies for work at the Dutch Colonial Trading company. They seek a letter of reference for him, and below is the letter they receive.

27 March 1936

H. Schotel

To: Dutch-Colonial Trading co. Ltd
Heerengracht 422

Amsterdam Centrum

Re. Requested Letter of Reference

Dear Sirs:

In reply to your letter of March 26 about Mr. Jac. Bebelaar, we can say that he does his work excellently. Also, he puts in extra hours after office hours to make sure that all his tasks are done. We therefore strongly recommend him.

Signed,

Yours truly
H. Schotel

Soon after, Jaap is presented an opportunity with the German firm, N.V. Carl Schlieper Trade Me, a manufacturer of high-quality knives. They need accounting staff for their operations in the Dutch East Indies. In April of 1936, Jaap starts his training at the German company's headquarters in Remscheid, Germany. Jaap travels by train and writes to Bé about his trip.

Remscheid, 5 April 1936

My sweetest wife,

As I promised you, I am writing you right away. Until Dusseldorf I was all by myself in the train compartment and amused myself with the the Haagse Post (journal). The trip was quite boring. Only the customs officer brought some variation. In Zevenaar an officer came to inspect my luggage and when I asked for a proof of my camera, I had to go out to the office. The train only stopped momentarily, and I had to run to get back on the train. The office could not give me the proof either, so I had to leave the camera behind and they will forward it to me later. It is a pity, because the surroundings here are very pretty, and I could have taken some nice pictures. In Emmerich I had to register my Dutch money at the German customs. Another diversion!

In Dusseldorf I had to transfer to a miserable local train, but finally I did arrive at my hotel. It is big and antique with many sculptures, real German. In the local train I had quite a conversation with the conductor. He showed me some nice spots and told me particulars about the area.

Arrived at the hotel. I tidied up somewhat and then went for dinner: "veal chops, potatoes and peas" with a cup of coffee and a glass of Pils. It was good, but they didn't offer gravy.

And now I am sitting and writing to you. Not much news but tomorrow that will be different. I will write you again, honey.

Many kisses and a big hug, your Jaap

The following day, Jaap spends his first day in the office for his training. He is understandably nervous and excited at the same time. The nerves he initially feels quickly turn into confidence, not only with his accounting abilities, but with his proficiency in the German language. The following letter was partially written in German.

Remscheid, 6th April 1936

My Dearest wife,

"Here come the camels"

I have experienced so much today that I don't believe I have enough paper to write on. To start at the beginning, yesterday I went to post the letter I wrote you, after which I took a stroll through Remscheid. Remscheid is situated at the top of a mountain (or a hill maybe) and city hall is at its highest point. The hotel is located significantly lower and therefore my tongue hit the street when I arrived at the market, which was not even the highest point yet! All beginnings are difficult, and I considered myself a great alpinist when I arrived there. There was nothing of great interest to do in the city, hence at 10:30 pm I was laying in "Morpeus' arms."

This morning I got up at 7 am, showered and shaved etc. etc., had breakfast and went to the firm at 9 am. That is at least half an hour walk outside of Remscheid in the village of Hasten, which is virtually attached to Remscheid. When I arrived, everyone was very friendly, and I first spent some time talking to Carl Toklieps. I took the opportunity to immediately ask him about my wage, but that will be agreed upon while I am here and when the other men agree with him hiring me.

After our talk he went to get the others: Walter Toklieps, his younger brother, and Mr. Felds, the head of accounting, a man like uncle Paul; an impressive, good-looking and well-spoken man. With him I went to the accounting department on the 2nd floor, where he gave me a brief but educational overview about the balance sheet etc. etc. This went very well.

Then Mr. Felds, the accountant, went to get Mr. Wüllenwebs, a man of approximately 40 years old who has quite a senior position within the firm. A very smart man but seems to prefer to do as little work as possible. He started off by showing me the accounts receivable ledger which overwhelmed me, and the more he talked the more it worried me. I had feared for this moment. He was called away for a moment and asked me to make a summary of what he had told me while he was away. I thought this was too difficult, hence I created an overview of how I would have done it myself, and as a result the air cleared and suddenly I understood what he has been telling me. I had just let myself get overwhelmed with the enormity of the task at hand, but it was no different than what I had in mind.

At noon Carl Toklieps came to have a look at what progress we had made. The accountant that initially had some doubts about my technical abilities, told him that we needed to discuss some additional new things in the afternoon and let him know that he had some ideas about what that would be. In the meantime, we had, as you call it, found each other, and just before going home, he told me all kinds of interesting facts. We said our goodbyes as two good old friends.

At 2 pm we started again, and we discussed additional items. Occasionally, he asked one of the girls to demonstrate something that we had been talking about (there are only girls here, of which 3 are completely separated and dedicated to accounts receivable and payable, which is where I sat for a while as well), while he was enjoying himself by occasionally tickling or stroking the girls' hair, which they seemed to enjoy very much. They are not very shy here when it comes to that; but they have a great sense of urgency when you ask them to do something, real German-Girls. I mean nothing with my terminology for the girls.

Before I went home I helped him with his work that needed to be done today. Carl Toklieps will not be at the office tomorrow morning, which is why he would go over the same thing with me again tomorrow morning. I don't have to start work at 7:15 am tomorrow, because at that time he has no work for me to do. He asked me to come to the office around 8:30 am. And tomorrow afternoon Carl Toklieps and I will finish some work at the office, which is why I might be at home on Wednesday.

Now my girl, I am in love (Oh, I received a lot of compliments for the fact that they think my German is so good – when I told them that I had not practiced my German very much in the past 8 years – nobody believed me – I was not even looking for ways to express myself).

What do you think of that?

I am looking forward to a letter from you my wife, and lots of kisses and a hug (and maybe also looking forward to asparagus with veal and mushrooms) from you,

Jaap

Give everyone at home my best regards!

It's already too late to write and I can't get any more postcards either.

I wrote Kor!

Also, happy birthday!

XXXX

XXXX

XX

Jaap returns home the next day. Life gets very busy. He has a new job and is leaving for it very quickly. He takes the train from Rotterdam to Utrecht, a city in Central Netherlands, approximately 64 km east of Rotterdam. From Utrecht he is to take a train to Italy, and then board a ship for the trip to the Dutch East Indies.

Jaap and Bé departing Rotterdam for Utrecht, April 1936. Last picture of Jaap in Holland.

Bé accompanies Jaap to Utrecht. They say their goodbyes on April 23, with the anticipation of reuniting in the Dutch East Indies. Until that time, they will communicate by letter, making plans for their life together.

Milan, 24 April 1936

My sweetest girl,

As we had said, I am sending you this note from Genoa. We now stand at the Milan station, so I am starting to write now. The largest part of the train trip is now done. It was beautiful. The trip along the south part of the Rhine is really very special. In Basel, the sleeping cars were attached, but nobody wanted to use them. Since our compartment was almost full we did not sleep very well, but it did not matter to me, because now I have seen Switzerland and North Italy, albeit in the dark. It really is fantastic. The compartment companions are not bad. I talked with the two Indo's that you saw yesterday. They are nice guys. In Arnhem yesterday two others joined us, one a draftsman with the BPM (oil company) in Balikpapan (Borneo), stayed in Borneo 18 years and is 12 years married. The other is a ship machinist with the Java-China-Japan Line, rather indifferent but we had a lot of fun together. That is what happened so far.

My dear wife, I thought of you all day. You are my brave girl. We have to be good and brave until we are back together in a little while. It won't be long now my girl. I will try to write more when we arrive in Genoa before I go on board of the ship. For now, many kisses and a big hug in thought,

Your Jaap.

Later this day, the train arrives in Genoa, and Jaap boards the *Marnix van St. Aldegonde*.

As Jaap promised, he writes to Bé later this day, before the ship departs.

Genoa, 24 April 1936

At 10 O'clock the train arrived in Genoa, and we went aboard. The trip from Milan to Genoa was beautiful. The station at Milan is huge. We got a breakfast there, two hard rolls with a slice of lamb's meat and roast beef along with a drink that they called coffee. The landscape looks a little Dutch except that we saw in the distance an enormous view of snowcapped Alpine peaks and also some kind of rice "sawahs." A little later we saw the spurs of the Apenine mountains and more Alps. Then it became really beautiful. Every so often the train went through a tunnel that sometimes took a few minutes and then again, the most magnificent view.

The ship is beautiful and luxurious. I am curious because everyone says that the best still has to come when we are sailing, and it is quiet at sea. My stateroom is quite roomy, a double bed for myself, so I can manage all right. I am one deck below the promenade deck, 1st and 2nd class. This afternoon at 2 pm the ship will start, so I can write to you now. Later I will take a photo of the cabin and also of Genoa.

Now my sweetheart, I will now stop. Every day I go further away but my thoughts are just as fast in Holland and I think of you. I will write in the first place where we land but that may take a little while. I also long for a letter from you. I will send some photos from Port Said when we arrive there.

My Bébetje, many kisses and a big hug from your Jaap

Jaap is now aboard the Marnix. His longing for his fiancé grows, as he now starts using cute terms of endearment, referring to her as Bébetje. He will now start meeting other passengers, some of whom will become important in his life in the years to come.

Mediterranen, 25 April 1936

My lovely girl,

Today I will write further to you, so at Port Said you get a romance in series. On board, it is just unbelievable, so luxurious and comfortable. Later I will take pictures of everything and also the cabin, so you can see for yourself. But first I will tell you about the boys that I see every day. In the train in Utrecht I had already acquainted the Indo you also saw in the train with his girl. His name is Corsten and he is mate on the KPM (Indonesian shipline). He is with a friend, Voogel, also a mate. And another boy is Henk Moddemeyer from The Hague who goes to a rubber plantation in Sumatra. He has a cabin beside mine, so we see each other regularly. We keep the door between us open, so we can talk to each other.

The food on board is fantastic. Last night we had hors d'oeuvres, soup, fish fillets with potatoes, roast beef, endive, Russian omelette and fruit. What a dinner! We sit at the same table with the four of us. That is nicer. You can also eat a la carte and then make your own choice.

Yesterday I went swimming with Henk on the Lido deck. There were some other people in the pool and also some on the side. Last night I slept very well and am now in good shape. Last night we also played bridge, but two still had to learn it. So, we decided to play for an hour every day, so they can learn. We also get served tea and coffee in the morning and afternoon. At the afternoon tea you can choose between all kinds of different types. They also come with a wagon with pastries and other tidbits. You just have to say it and you get it. And after dinner also coffee first and after an hour tea with more tidbits. What a service. The service by the Javanese waiters and cabin boys is also fantastic. I tried to talk with the cabin boy and tipped him with a few guilders. He then promised to bring tea or coffee to my bed and also shine my shoes every day.

So tomorrow I will write further. Are you still going to the film with Nel? For now, many kisses and a big hug. I loved your letter that came in Genoa.

Jaap has made a promise to send a series of romance letters from Port Said.

Monday, 27 April 1936

My little wife,

Yesterday, I didn't have a chance to write. Saturday night there was a ball on board. There was a lot of dancing. But as grass widowers we just sat in a corner and were watching it. In the afternoon we had passed the Stromboli volcano. It was quite something to see. A wisp of smoke came from the crater, while you could see where the lava had been around it. We were a few hundred meters away from it and on one side there was a small village that you could see. I would not want to live on the side of an active volcano. In the evening we sailed through the Strait of Messina. That was fantastic. The city lies against a mountain and beside it you could see the lights of little villages. Last night we passed the isle of Crete. It was dark, but there was a blinking light that looked like lightning. That was the farewell to Europe. A strange feeling that I am now out of our old continent.

Yesterday, Sunday morning at 7 o'clock we went sporting for an hour. That was fine. After that we had breakfast and then we did some deck-games, golf, quoits and deck- tennis. It was nice and you really need the movement to keep fit. You eat like a prince. The breakfast is so extensive with eggs, cereal, all kinds of sandwiches, nasi goreng, fruits, too much to name it all. Here you always eat a la carte. At noon an extensive warm or cold lunch and to top it all off a scrumptious dinner. So, you really get spoiled. When you come later you must definitely take 2nd class. I definitely don't want anything else for you.

Last night they had a movie in 1st class. First a news journal, then a Betty Boop film and finally a Laurel and Hardy film. It was hilarious. We also played bridge yesterday, so I couldn't write you. Now my angel, tomorrow my last letter and then we are in Port Said. I long for a letter from you, even more long for yourself. It would have been nice if you already could have come along with me. Many big, big kisses from your Jaap.

Tomorrow morning at 6 we will be in Port Said. Immediately after mooring the mail will be distributed. I look out for your letter. I also am busy now with the Malay language. In the beginning it is difficult to learn all those new words, many look alike. But the structure is simple, no declensing, no articles, etc. Some servants speak a little Dutch or English, but not all of them and then I have to use gesture language. My cabin boy says every morning "Goede morgen Tuan" (that is sir). You definitely have to go to that school in The Hague where they have things from the Indies and you also learn to speak. You will have a lot of use of that when you come. From Port Said I will only write a letter to you. To home I will send a postcard. How did your father make out in Brabant this week? I am very curious. Greet Mamma and father and the boys. You can tell them something from this letter. Now my darling, many firm kisses and a big hug in thought from your Jaap.

I really wish my father would have read this letter. Growing up not knowing his father, it would have been such an important moment in his life to find a connection to him. Reading that Jaap and his friends took to golf onboard ship, would have been monumental for my father. My dad took up the game of golf in the 1960s, and to my knowledge, never knew of his father's tinkering with the game. When I read this, it was the first I had ever heard of this connection to the game.

The following day, the ship arrives at Port Said, in Egypt. Jaap sends his trilogy of romance letters, after writing one more this day. This is not a stop that he enjoys, but this Port will become an important stop in the passage of family members in the years to come.

Suez, 28 April 1936

My sweetest Bébetje,

It was so nice to read your long letter this morning. While you wrote it on the day that I left, it was good that you still could catch the train at 10 o'clock and that you could get some sleep at home, so you were well rested. You have to be fit and well when you come later. Oh, my little wife, I must not think of that moment we had to part, it was terrible. But we must carry on as best as we can and that will be harder for you, because I have much diversion that you have not.

It was nice that Gerda also wrote to you. Did you also write back to Piet and Dini?

About life on board I wrote already in my last letter. As far as spending money, I didn't spend more than fl 3 and that includes fl 2 that I paid for a sweepstake. You had to guess how many miles per day the ship sailed. But that is enough, for the rest you cannot spend much on board, everything is free. There is a complete shop, like a small Bijenkorf (general store) on a small scale.

Your letter I mailed last night when we moored in Port Said. We arrived at 6 in the morning and we let ourselves be called at 5 so that we could see the mooring of the ship along the quay.

We were from 6 to 10 ashore in Port Said but what a dirty and degenerated people there are. You just have no idea what dogs these Arabs are; you can't find a better word for it. They steal like ravens and are such miserable people that my pen just cannot describe them. They speak a little of different languages, but you can hardly understand them. They storm you with as many as 20 and try to sell you anything. One sells cigarettes, another all dirty things that I did not even know existed, a third will be a guide, a fourth is just a beggar and you can hardly get rid of them. I snarled at them the best I could. That is the easiest, but they just don't give up. One guy walked half the town with us and called us "meneer the gravin" (Mister Countess). At the end he looked at us with a desperate face and said, "Mister Baron" and "Mister Count," all in broken Dutch. We laughed hard at him. Voogel gave him a penny and said in Dutch, "Rot up" but it didn't help, and he continued to walk with us!

We then went to the well-known Simon Arzt, a big superstore where you can buy anything and not very expensive. Films were only 36 cts, cameras, dress shirts, etc. I bought a pith helmet for only fl 2.70 and very stylish. Most passengers did the same.

And what is very interesting are the fakirs. One was admitted on board and sat on our deck. He had a little baby chick that ran around and a beaker he placed upside down on the ground so that you could see that it was empty. He then put the beaker on the ground, makes a chicken-sound and lifts the beaker under which there now is an egg. He takes the egg, beats it against his head and breaks it and then it is changed into a baby-chick. He then puts 3 chicks in his hand, squeezes it and then it is one chick. It is really unbelievable. You have to see it. Other people dive for money which is also quite something. One guy managed to stay on board as a stow-away. A ship's officer came to force him to dive off the deck. He cried and prayed to Allah to allow him some dimes, after which he dove from the 18-meter high deck. You can't have pity for these guys. If they have a chance they'll steal you blind. All hatches and portholes had to be locked while we were there.

I found cigarillos and cigarettes in my suitcase, which was nice because I smoke more now with my friends. There also was a large parcel in the suitcase with nothing on it. I took the paper off but didn't look any further because I suspect it to be for my birthday, so I wrapped it up again. It would be a pity if there is no letter from you in Colombo, but at least we are then over the half and then I will get regular mail from you, right my dear? We now are floating on the Bitterlakes. It is very beautiful.

Well my little wife, my warm greetings for Father, Mamma, your father and mams, etc., etc. and yourself a big kiss and a big hug from your Jaap

Red Sea, 2 Mei 1936

My sweetest Bébetje,

Today I will start a new letter to you. You hadn't thought that you might get a letter from Suez. It was just at the last minute that the mailboat could take it along. How did you like the pictures that I had included? I will send more pictures later on. And how are you, so alone? Is it busy at van Dijk? And in the evening, you will also be busy with all kinds of things. You know, I started to inquire how expensive it is to furnish a house in the Indies. My mate Corsten also wants to have his girlfriend come over next year. He says it is about fl 900 to furnish a house reasonably. That is not so bad. don't you think? It may look like a lot of money, but I will also look for bargains once I am there. You know, my little wife, I only spent about fl 12.50 this first week on board and that includes the pith helmet, the tip to the cabin boy and the sweepstake ticket. So, I think fl 25 will cover the whole trip. The weather in Holland is still rather droopy. We get the ships journal every afternoon with all the news from Holland. While I am writing to you I use the big fan to keep it cool and at night I turn it to half speed. Tuesday, we had another movie night. A Laurel and Hardie movie with a lot of slapstick. Wednesday, we had a bridge-drive cost fl 1. I played with Voogel, but we didn't win. Last night we had a great Orange Souper in honour of HRH Princess Juliana. I will include the menu so you can see. After the supper there was a roulette-ball, together with the first class. That was nice. Only most people showed up in tuxedo or jacquette, very chique and formal. But the four of us were just in our cotton and linen suits. Voogel and Corsten danced, but I did not. At the end they handed out some souvenirs which I will send to you.

We now have a regular daily routine: sporting, reading, games and bridge, etc. Tonight, there will be a concert. Well my sweet girl, tomorrow we will be in the Indian Ocean and it will be a little cooler. I think often of you, my angel. Many kisses from your Jaap.

5 May 1936

My angel,

We finished our daily tasks and now I will write to you. This morning we first took pictures, then we swam. After lunch we played bridge for a couple of hours, every day a little longer. The concert last night was not much, the program was old numbers that they had rehearsed the night before. After that there were deck-horse races. That was quite interesting. A racetrack was set up on the verandah deck with ropes and flags. Around it you sat or stood. The horses were made of triplex and had a number and a name.

You then bought a lottery ticket for fl 1, and then the horses were raffled out. The "owner" of a horse chose a lady who would be the "jockey." She got a paper jockey cap. When it was your turn, you tossed a die which decided the number of places the horse would move. You can also bet on the winning horse for 50 cts. There were 4 races. The owner of the winning horse gets fl 20. With the 4 of us we won fl 2. The net surplus of all the races goes to the Lifeboat Association, as a charity.

Last night there was a concert from the Marnix-Singers. A choir made up of crew members, stewards, pursers, chefs, etc. That was quite nice. They had good voices although with some Amsterdam accent. All in all, it was a successful evening. Voluntary donations from the public yielded fl 58, for a good purpose.

We also had another movie night "Naughty Marietta" with Jeanette MacDonald, quite a nice film. While I am looking at my watch I see it is 11 o'clock in the morning in Holland right now while here it is 4 o'clock in the afternoon. Peculiar, isn't it? You are probably just starting now at van Dijk. Tonight, we have to move our watches ahead one hour. But we don't go to bed any earlier. We don't sleep in the afternoon either. It is quite warm here in the Indian Ocean but not as humid as in the Red Sea. Every day is beautiful, not a cloud in the sky, but like a hot summer day in Holland. Every day I play my violin for half an hour. But then I perspire and have to put dry clothes on. I usually take a bath then and dry my clothes in front of the fan.

Last night one of the passengers gave a talk with slides from Java and especially about the Principalities of Jokjakarta and Surakarta. That was most beautiful. You just can't imagine how beautiful it is there. We will actually settle quite close to there and it will be nice to have our vacation there and also maybe our delayed honeymoon. Now, my Bébetje, if nothing comes in between, you will join me here next September; that must be possible. We will try to economize. It would be lovely if we could celebrate your birthday here together in our own home!! You should soon start with learning the language. It actually is not that difficult but is quite outside our notion of language. You just have to learn simple words like speak, bring, fetch, walk, lie down, go, where, there, etc. I can already help myself in talking to the cabin boy.

He can understand me, so when I called to him "Djongos, bawah handdoek" (bring a towel) he knew. I will send you a picture of my faithful servant, Matatoeli, it is a nice guy. Every morning he wakes me up with a "kopi". That is coffee (the inlanders cannot say the letter f and say p instead). Eating and drinking is quite different here. At lunch there is no bread, but always something warm. I will send you a few menus. Oh yes, I didn't tell you yet about the white-suit parade!

In the Red Sea passengers started to wear their tropical suits, all in white. It was such a strange sight those first few days. It is a festive idea, real gay! But after a few days you get used to it and you would find it strange if you saw someone in a dark suit. It is also the custom to dress better for the lunch and with the evening meal most ladies dress long and men wear tuxedos or dinner jackets. People on the ship are usually quiet. They don't do funny things or spend a lot of money. But at 5 pm there is always "happy hour" and they drink Dutch gin but not excessively and everyone behaves.

Tonight, there will be a costume-ball and I am curious to see how that will go. Tomorrow afternoon we arrive in Colombo and I look forward to your letter. I haven't heard from you in so long and saw nothing but sea and air. It is nice. Once I am in Indie we can write more frequently (with the airmail). With my letter, I will include some more pictures. I am beginning to get used to the camera.

P.S. It is now half past 3 at night. I just had a bath and write now in my pyjamas. The costume ball was over at 2 am. It was quite nice. Some costumes were quite original. The ship gave a prize to the most beautiful ladies-costume. There was also a champagne bar that was used a lot. Henk and I also took one glass. It was delicious, but I also noticed in my wallet. It was 75ct per glass. Is that O.K. my wifey? I also enclose a few pictures I took. On the back you'll see what they are. Will you give my greetings to Father, Mamma and other friends and family? Many kisses and a warm hug from your Jaap.

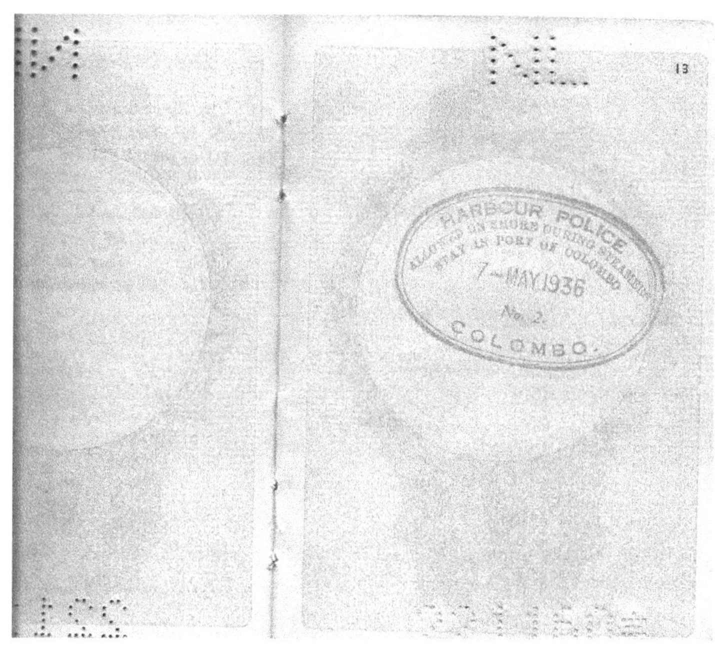

Indian Ocean, 8 May 1936

My sweetest girl,

It was nice to have your letter in Colombo yesterday! It made my day. Father's letter was there too. It is so great when you are so far away from home and then you get a letter. You just can't imagine. Yesterday I mailed an airmail letter to you from Colombo. The letter I am writing now will be mailed from Belawan, Sumatra. You may get those at the same time. I am now wearing sunglasses. It is very nice on your eyes because the sun is so bright. As far as the heat goes I have no problem with that, but I do take an occasional bath in the "mandibak" (a sort vertical bathtub) to keep cool, especially before dinner, because then you have to dress properly.

With the four of us we have a nice little club. We do everything together and the other passengers call us the "bachelors club," but we always behave very correctly. We don't meddle much with other passengers and mind our own business. We also don't flirt as others do. Also, girls who are married and on their way to their husbands still flirt. It is not as it should be. There are brides-to-be who fall in the arms of good looking ships officers. Don't you think that's pretty bad? How lucky I am with my little Bebetje! Last week at the costume ball we had an amusing case. There is a crazy German girl-passenger who also speaks English. She is "hot" on anything that is a man. She obviously had so much champagne that she hardly could stand on her legs. My friend Herman went to the deck at 3 o'clock in the night and found this girl in warm embrace with her "friend." Herman said, "Is nobody here to carry you to your cabin?" She said, "The domestic worker will carry me." And then her "friend" says, "I am the domestic worker," picks her up, carries her away, disappears with her in the cabin and doesn't come out any more. What do you think of that?

It's nice that you could get a room for fl 20, and also that you could keep the piano. I will try to make it as short as possible. I continue practicing on my violin. I stop now but will add more lines before Belawan and tell you more things about Colombo. Many kisses my sweet wife.

9 May.

My honeybun, how sweet you are, my angel. This morning the steward came with your telegram for my birthday. Of course, you celebrate today in thought. After reading the telegram, I immediately opened the parcels that you put in the suitcase. What a beautiful photo album! I pasted the telegram on the first page. That is a nice memory. I hope to get some more pictures from you so that I can put them in. Henk Moddemeyer also congratulated me this morning. That was nice. The others don't know, but I will treat them tonight with a drink. Our club has expanded with a young just-married couple: Mr. and Mrs. Joha. They are from The Hague. He is with the BPM [Dutch Shell] as a draftsman and goes to Balikpapan in Borneo. That's where the BPM has oilfields, but it is in the middle of the jungle, and there are no other places where you can go to. They are both going there for the first time, so it takes some courage. But his salary and paid expenses make it worthwhile. He also gets 2 weeks vacation in Java and every 6 years, a six-month furlough in Holland. The salary is fl 500 per month and fl 1000 for furnishing expenses. It is a nice couple, and the 6 of us spend every night together.

And what a nice book you gave me. This morning I started to read it, and have it almost finished now. It is really special and there are things in there that relate directly to us together. It talked for instance about "suffering" and that is something quite natural for everybody in day-to-day life. Everyone will experience suffering in one way or the other. It comes out of nature and it is given us so that we can become a better person in the middle of our fellow men. It may sound somewhat sentimental, but when I read it I immediately had to think of the two of us. Right now we both have to suffer in order to make ourselves better, but surely, if we see it that way, it will make our married life stronger and happier. My little wife, I do believe that it will also widen your view of life and give you a new perspective. I say this not out of egoism but because I think that we have to do more in life than only pursue our own happiness. But we won't experience this "more of life" if we only think of ourselves (in our marriage I mean). My wifey, I have been a "tin pastor" again. Sorry.

Today we arrived at Sabang and to my great joy I found a whole pile of mail for my birthday. I loved that they all thought of me, and I will start to answer them all and send them by airmail. The boys are all really nice. I will treat them to a cigar. Last night we played bridge again and then I treated them to a drink.

You also asked what they are doing. Well, Hugo and Herman have been in Indie for 13 years, both as 2nd mate with the KPM. They came back from their furlough, Hugo for 9 months and Herman for 14 months of which he first sailed from China to San Francisco. He bought a car there and drove to his girl friend in Chicago. He then spent 5 months with her touring through the States. He then put the car on the Veendam of the HAL and sailed with his girl friend to Holland where his 70-year-old mother still lived. He stayed there for another 8 months but his mother died at that time, so he could still bury her. He just heard from the KPM that he has to go to Singapore. Hugo and I will continue to Batavia. Henk studied at the Tropical School in Deventer and goes to the Deli-Batavia-Company at the Tobameer, which is also in the jungle. So, our little club comes to an end. That is the way it goes. Well, we are slowly nearing our end destination and I am eager to get started in my new job.

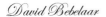

Sabang is a beautiful island, much nicer than other places we have seen. While in Colombo you were followed all the time by poor and pressing people who were trying to sell you something, the people in Sabang are quiet and pleasant. There is a wide bay with mountains in the background, all covered with large trees. When you walk, there are beautiful views everywhere. I took some pictures, which you will see later. Sabang is also a free port, so you can buy all kinds of things very cheaply: cologne, toiletries, shoes, shirts, etc., etc. I bought nice white linen shoes and also cigarettes. I also bought open slippers from buffalo leather; they are better than the old ones I had. It was only one rupiah (guilder). Hugo told me that in Indie as a bachelor you can live for fl 125 per month. If that is true then we should soon get married, my wifey. Now that I have heard more about the living conditions here it seems to me the best to get married by proxy. But I will write more about that later. I will now start writing the other letters. The one for Father and Mamma I will include in here, that is cheaper. In Belawan I will write a few more lines before mailing this. Many kisses and big hugs, your Jaap

P.S. We went swimming in the pool in Sabang. The water was 29 degrees Celcius, unbelievable. I will mail this letter now and will later write from Singapore. Bye my sweet girl.

Jaap writes to Bé about a "proxy wedding." This was a common occurrence at this time. For many, the rules were that you had to come to the Dutch East Indies as a "single" man. This is how Jaap arrived, although he was engaged to Bé. Under a proxy wedding (also known as a "white-glove wedding"), the father of the groom would stand in for the groom, the ceremony would take place, and the wedding would be official. The new wife would then travel to meet up with her husband in the Dutch East Indies.

Batavia, 15 May 1936

My sweetest wife,

After Belawan I did not write any further until now. In Belawan I got your letter and also a letter from Per in which he wrote that I would stay in Batavia for the time being. I had not expected that since I had not heard from Schlieper either. I didn't know what I would do. Also, in Singapore there was no letter from Schlieper, so I would have to wait until we arrive in Priok (port of Batavia). In Belawan, Henk M. was met by someone from his firm with a car. They first had to go to Medan to buy some furniture and after that they would drive by car some hundred miles further inland. He was overly nervous, and we had to say goodbye to him in a hurry. It was strange when he was gone. All the weeks on board we had had a good time together. We then went with the Joha's (she was a cousin of Groude who was an agent of your father) and Hugo and Herman by car to Medan. Medan is quite pretty. We drove for 3 to 4 hours for 5 Rupia with the three of us, so that wasn't expensive. Then another 28 km to Belawan. In Sabang, Herman had been told to proceed to Singapore, so we lost him there and bade him a warm farewell. He was a real nice guy! Thursday morning, we arrived in Priok. I did not see anybody on board, neither Eppie nor Dick Bontenbal, however there was a letter from the sister of Uncle Jan Radstaake with a welcome to Indie and an invitation to visit them as soon as I could. That was nice. Will you write me Eppie's address so that I possibly can visit him? And then there was your letter. How lovely! I had abandoned all hope but look there it was! It was marvelous my little girl. You really look for surprises even if it is far away!

In all the bustle on the quay after debarking I run into a gentleman who says, "Mr. Bebelaar? My name is Klinks from the Schlieper firm." How do you like that? It was a somewhat elderly gentleman. We immediately went to get my luggage from board, a car was waiting for us, we got in and drove away. 8 o'clock we had moored and half past 9 I sat in the car. At 9 we stopped in front of the Schlieper office on the Koningsplein (the main square in the centre of Batavia, about a square kilometer in area). The Schlieper office is an enormous building, must have cost about 1 ½ million.

For about an hour he took me around to present me to all the European staff and show me the whole building. Then we went to hotel Victoria. Klinks found the room price of fl 80 too high and started to negotiate. We now will get a 10% discount. At 11 o'clock I was already working until half past 12, after which we went to lunch. From 1:30 to 4:30 we worked again! They let you sort things out by yourself. The personnel consists of about 24 Europeans and

75 inlanders, so it took me some time. The office manager, Mr. Meulenbeld, a Dutchman, gave me a job to figure out something that the people in Remscheid nor in the other branch offices couldn't quite understand. If I had figured it out I had to tell him and explain it. At 3 o'clock I had found it and had to find the application in the balance of Jan. 1, 1935. The next morning, I continued with it and discovered that the new system that had been adopted in 1934 had not been applied at the first balance! When I told him this he was utterly surprised, started to figure and calculate and concluded that I was absolutely correct, so then I had to make all the corrections together with the Chinese bookkeeper.

For the rest of the day, I just had control work and that will continue until in June, the boss, Mr. Schlemmer, will go on 6 months furlough. I will then take over part of Meulenbeld's work. They mean business here, but fortunately I get along nicely with Meulenbeld, so I hope that everything will turn out all right. I haven't yet met Mr. Paul Schlieper who was in Semarang for a few days. Tomorrow he will be back. You know, when I checked the balance I came across an account I did not understand. When I asked Meulenbeld he told me that it was an account of savings made by the personnel. Every employee is allowed to deposit money in there and get a 6% interest!!! What do you think of that? Let me know. I will soon be sending money to you so you can pay all our debts and after that we should put our savings in this account.

Next time I will write more about the hotel and the life here. Tomorrow this letter will go. Wasn't it nice for Henk and Corrie? Congratulate them from me. I will write them. Many kisses and a tropical hug from your boy Jaap. Give my greetings to your and my parents. I will write them the next time. Last night I went to the film; tonight, Hugo will come for a visit.

Bye my dear

Many kisses from your Jaap

Below is the passenger list of the *Marnix van St. Aldegonde*, as was published in the *Bataviaash Niewsblad* on April 24, 1936. The ship departs Amsterdam on April 15, but Jaap boards the ship when it arrives in Genoa, Italy.

Delpher

De Sumatra post

02-05-1936

PASSAGIERS.

Passagiers van het m.s. „Marnix van St. Aldegonde", 15 April van Amsterdam vertrokken en 11 Mei te Belawan verwacht.

P. W. Aalbersberg, Mevr. J. J. Aarse en 2 kinderen, J. Ackroyd Stuart, Mevr. F. Akkermans en kind, fam. H. van Amerongen, A. S. Andersen, Mevr. A. N. van Ark, Rev. Father B. Ashness, N. Bakker, fam. L. Barreau, fam. J. J. C. de Bas en 2 kinderen, J. Bebelaar, J. van den Berg, Mevr. J. A. Best, W. Blankert, Mej. W. J. F. Boissevain, Ir. P. A. Bömer, fam. J. C. L. Boosman en 2 kinderen, C. J. Bosman, Mej. A. L. H. Brouwer, fam. P. de Bruyn, Mej. M. S. A. Busch, I. M. Bijleveld, Mej. K. M. Carey, fam. F. A. Celosse en 5 kinderen, H. A. Corsten, The Rt. Hon. Viscountess St. Davids, Dr. W. L. Davids, Jonkvr. A. W. Dedel. fam. H. A. Dikmans

<u>Bataviaash Niewsblad, April 24, 1936</u>

Marnix van St. Aldegonde

Captain: B. A. Potjer

Passengers on the m.s. *Marnix van St.* Aldegonde left Amsterdam April 15 and are expected to arrive in Belawan [Dutch East Indies] May 11: P. W. Aalbersberg, Mrs. J. J. Aarse and 2 children, J. Ackroyd Stuart, Mrs. F. Akkermans and child, fam. H. van Amerongen, A. S. Andersen, Mrs. A. N. van Ark, Rev. Father B. Ashness, N. Bakker, fam. L. Barreau, fam. J. J. C. de Bas and 2 children, **J. Bebelaar**, J. van den Berg, Mrs. J. A. Best, W. Blankert, Miss W. J. F. Boissevain, Engineer P. A. Bomer, fam. J. C. L. Boosman and 2 children, C. J. Bosman, Miss A. L. H. Brouwer, fam. P. de Bruyn, Miss M. S. A. Busch, I. M. Bijleveld, Miss K. M. Carey, fam. F. A. Celosse and 5 children, **H.A. Corsten**, The Rt. Hon. Viscountess St. Davids, Dr. W. L. Davids, Lady A. W. Dedel, fam. H. A. Dikmans and 2 children, A. M. M. Donners, fam. W. E. B. Dunningham, P. W. Duson, Mrs. de Wed. A. Elshove, fam. A. A. Epker, fam. I. F. Esser and 3 children, fam. J. A. A. Essink, Dr. Falck, Mrs. J. J. Florin, fam. Mr. H. A. Flothuis and child, Miss H, Fokkema, H. Fonteyn and son,

J. L. Fuhren, Miss A. de Geit, Mrs. C. J. van Ginkel, fam. A. N. Gmelig Meyling, K. Groot, Mrs. G. H. A. van Gulik and child, V. Haffenden, A. M. Hage, fam. A. Hamming and 4 children, W. J. Hanekuijk, fam. Engineer G. A. van der Harst and 2 children, C. den Hartoog, fam. N. J. H. van Hasselt and child, fam. W. Hent, fam. P. A. M. Heuperman and 4 children, H. J. van der Hilst, Miss E. J. M. Hochstenbach, fam. E. G. Hoefer and child, H. Hoekstra, A. Hoet, Miss J. M. Hojel, Mrs. E. Holl, fam. Engineer P. A. J. de Hon and 3 children, J. H. M. van der Hooft, fam. S. J. G. Hoop and child, Mrs. F. Houk, Miss G. P. Huisman, fam. M. A. Huysmans, Enigneer A. C. Ingeneren, fam. M. van Iperen, Mrs. de Wed. Th. J. C. Israel-Chalmers Hoynck van Papendrecht, Mrs. M. C. F. Jansen and 2 children, Miss G. Jenken, H. J. M. Jochems, **fam. G. Joha**, J. P. de Josselin de Jong, fam. J. V. Kamerling, Mrs. A. H. Kass, Miss E. Kastner, Miss A. Kehlenbrink, fam. van der Kleyn and child, W. R. Knaap, C. P. Th. Koch and child, fam. Lord H. G. de Kock and 4 children, fam. W. J. Koert and 6 children, fam. K. Kooy, J. Koster, Mr. B. L. Kroon and 2 children, fam. J. W. Labberté, fam. D. J. Landzaal and 3 children, Mrs. C. A. Leepel and 2 children, fam. A. J. D. Lepez and 5 children, fam. E. Letsche and 3 children, Mrs. E. M. M. G. Leurs and 4 children, fam. F. J. M. van Liempt and child, fam. J. Ligthelm and child, A. H. J. Lombert Jr., fam. Th. J. Maagdenberg and child, fam. J. Malasch and 3 children, Miss E. Meevers, W. Meinesz Lzn, Drs. R. L. Mellema and 2 children, **J. H. Moddemeyer**, H. Moes, Mrs. Moes and 3 children, Miss U. C. Morant, fam. E. B. Mulder Jr., F. W. Muller, J. Nijhof, P. A. van den Oever, J. C. Oltmans, P. Omes, fam. W. G. van Oyen and 2 children, fam. H. A. F. Paproth, Th. J. Peelen, The Hon. Miss L. Phillips, Mrs. J. F. Pieterse, Mrs. W. H. P. M. Pilger, Mrs. C. M. W. van der Poel, Mrs. B. Potjer and child, W. S. J. A. Prins, fam. F. H. E. Rapmund and child, Mrs. G. van Ravenhorst, fam. N. P. Rawlins, fam. D. J. Rigterink and son, F. W. H. Roessel, J. W. de Roo, fam. P. L. de Rooy and 3 children, J. P. Rotgans, Mrs. J. F. Th. Ruesink, fam. D. Ruyer and child, H. W. Rijk, H. Salm, Mrs. J. H. M. Sandkuijl and child, fam. D. Scalongne, fam. Dr. P. J. van der Schaar and 4 children, J. Scheenhart, J. Scheenhart, fam. G. M. Scholten and 2 children, Mrs. J. Schoneman, A. F. H. Schrijvers, R. W. Schuepp and child, fam. W. Schuitema, C. Schulte, W. de Silva and 2 children, fam. Ds. G. J.

Sirks, C. de Smalen, fam. H. Smits and child, fam. H. J. Snoep and 3 children, Raden Soekarjo, L. Sonnenberg, Miss H. M. Spook, J. Staal, H. D. Stibbe, Mrs. N. J. van Suchtelen, Mrs. P. Swager and child, Miss. L. Swart, Mrs. de Wed G. G. Teerink, D. Tegelaar, W. Q. Telfer, fam. D. Terpstra, Theé Bing Tjiauw, Mrs. M. C. Thomas, A. Tichler, Mrs. A. G. Timmermans and child, P. A. van Toorenenbergen, Miss J. A. van Tricht, M. F. Tydeman, W. Uytenbroek, fam. A. P. Varekamp, C. Varkevisser, fam. Q. de Veer, J. van de Velde, Mr. A. G. Veldhuis and 2 children, Mrs. C. Verboeket, fam. Mr. K. F. J. Verboeket and child, fam. G. C. Verhaert and 2 children, C. A. Vermolen, H. L. Verniers van der Loeff, fam. H. Verschuur and child, R. Versteeg, Mrs. M. J. Vischer-Prince, Miss J. H. Vleeming, A. J. ter Voert, fam. A. Voigt and 2 children, **H. A. Voogel**, N. C. Voorhout, J. de Vries, J. H. de Vries, fam. Ir. G. S. Vrijburg and 3 children, L. W. Walraven, Mrs. A. van der Wateren, Dr. F. Weber, J. G. Weenink, A. Weiss, Mrs. A. P. Wentholt and 2 children, Mrs. C. C. Werlingshoff and child, W. L. Wesselo and 2 children, Mrs. J. C. M. van Weynsbergen, Jongenh. G. W. van Wezel, fam. L. C. Wilhelm and child, Mrs. O. A. van Wijk, fam. J. Wijnen Riems, J. Zaayer, E. A. Zeilinga, Mrs. W. F. C. Zur Mühlen.

(Source: «Gevonden Op Delpher - De Sumatra Post.» Delpher.nl. Accessed August 19, 2018. https://www.delpher.nl/nl/kranten/view?query=J. Bebelaar&facets[periode][]=2|20e_eeuw|1930-1939|1937|&page=1&coll=ddd&identifier=ddd:010383743:mpeg21:a0181&resultsidentifier=ddd:010383743:mpeg21:a0181)

Batavia, 17 May 1936

My dearest girl,

My last letter was written in haste, so I didn't tell many details. Everything here is so new and peculiar for me that I could write ten pages and still would forget half of it. Yet I sit here now as if I have been here all my life. My neighbour in the hotel came yesterday to get acquainted. He is a geological engineer from Delft and asked me how many years I had already been here. When I asked him where he got that idea, he said that he found me acting so normal as though nothing was new to me!

The room in the hotel is just so-so, not fancy, but I can live in it. A big bed with a "klamboo" (mosquito net), a fixed wash-stand, a closet with a large mirror, a table and chair and an arm chair. The walls are painted yellow. Outside there is a small terrace with a round table, chair and a lazy chair. Also, a large desk with a chair. Further some pots with palms in them. All right at the street. The office is about 5 minutes walking from here, so that is not bad.

Per had ordered some flowers to place on my table, so that made it homey. I could see, for that matter, that he enjoyed the company of an old acquaintance. I think he actually is somewhat homesick. Rather down, troubled by the heat because he does not perspire. Don't tell this to Nel. I think he's rather lax. I hadn't thought that of him. He drinks a lot of beer and whiskey, especially because of the heat and that shows up in your wallet. Life is also more expensive than in Holland. I told him that he should slow down with his expenses, but he just laughs about it. His marriage plans also are not very serious and when I sounded him out about that he said that he didn't give it much thought. He also did not save much, went twice a week to the movies which is fl 1.25 each time. Last night I joined him, but not the second time. I do spend some money but then also want to save for our wedding later. I had a talk yesterday with Meulenbeld, the office manager, and told him that I planned to get married next year. He said that was a good idea but warned me that I should know who to marry. A lot of marriages here failed after a few years, often because of a "house friend" or wild parties. I told him that in our case it was quite in order and we did not have to worry about that. I also deposited fl 80 in the company's savings account yesterday, rather than keep it in my room. Furthermore, I made inquiries what would be the best to do when you come here next year. We would live for a few months in a hotel; there are good hotels with 2-person rooms for about fl 120 per month, everything included.

In that time, you can acclimatize and also get used to the people here because in the beginning you will find it a little strange. Another good idea I heard is to bring drawings of the furniture you want to have. You can give this to a Chinese furniture maker who will make it very cheaply. Hugo asked the price for a dining room, bedroom, office, rattan terrace furniture at a European furniture store and it was about fl 120, all together. But at the Chinese it will be some 20% less. So, what do you think? Anyway, write me your thoughts about this. How lovely it will be when you are here with me! What I don't like is that we eat dinner at 8 at night while you are already home at half past 4. Once we are in our own home we will change that. Well Bebetje, tomorrow I write again. At 5 this afternoon I visit Mrs. Jo Bergkamp, the sister of Uncle Jan Radstaake. Many kisses! Your Jaap

Batavia, 11 September 1936

My dearest girl,

How courageous you are to decide right away to have a tooth extracted. You are a real brave girl! So now your teeth are O.K. again. I never realized that we already are over half of our time of separation. I wonder how long it will take before you have all the papers so that we can get married. So much red tape involved to get us married. I also had expected a letter from Mamma and Father, was curious to see what they thought now that our plans are becoming more solid. I hope that they can get used to the idea that you will be so far away from them. I still remember the discussions we had with Mamma when we talked over our future, that we did not know much and yet that I wanted to leave. Oh, my girl, five years will pass quickly. The most important thing I find yet that we will be happy, not only for myself but also for them and I assure you that if you can stand the climate you will have a life as a princess, my angel. I always have been a great optimist, thought that we could make it all right, yet I hadn't thought that I could take you so soon in my arms as my wife. You'll see that you will really like it! Only I don't want to become a real colonial, but anyway I don't think we have a tendency for that.

You know, Bebetje that we are still in a festive mood here because of the engagement of Princess Juliana and Prince Bernhard. On Wednesday we got off at 11 in the morning. And Saturday being the official celebration, will also be a holiday. All offices in the Centre are illuminated or decorated. Our office has a big floodlight in front. And next Wednesday will be a day off when the new governor general will arrive and be installed. So, we are celebrating all the time, but I wish you were here to celebrate with me!! Alone I don't care so much about it.

Say, Bebetje, I actually hated myself after I read your letter with your comments about the N.M.B. (Nederlandce Middenstands Bank?). Did I fret too much about it? Did you find me a bore? I wish I hadn't written about it. In a letter you can't always express yourself. I sometimes cannot think logical and am mad at myself and that drove me to write to you about it. But, we will be quieter when we are married and always together. I couldn't stand it without you my little wife. I am sure that together we will be madly in love and I will remain my whole life in love with you, really in love, my wifey. That when we are 80 we still can do and be as when we were engaged. And that we can really feel it, my Bebetje, didn't we have a lovely engagement time? I often still think of the first time we met at the St. Nicholas party on the Math Way, and I took your arm for the first time. I sang and shouted for joy. After that the evenings at Andersen and the walks we made in the park on Saturday nights and the night that we agreed to become one. After all it looked so childlike, but it was lovely. After that we became more adult and became officially engaged! You then begin to feel important and grown-up. What a smashing party it turned out to be! And in spite of everything, in spite of almost being married, I still feel myself thus: childlike and madly in love with my loveliest future wife!!! (How does that sound?) While I write this I still really don't know. Do I dream or is it really true that you are my wife and I am your husband? I am actually much too childlike for that, at least that is the way it feels. But how much experience have we gained meanwhile! My dear wifey, I believe that just that childlike feeling we have that that is the most important happiness we have, and that if we ever will have a child ourselves, what will make us the happiest is that together with our child we remain a child ourselves!

My Bebetje, I digressed in thought, but I must finish now because the letter will have to go tonight. I loved it that I could really speak with you. I really need that, to be pampered by you, even if it is only on paper. I always think of you! Many warm kisses and a big hug from your boy, Jaap

In anticipation of leaving the Netherlands for the Dutch East Indies, Bé starts to gather documentation she feels she will need, in hopes of obtaining work in her new home. She receives the following reference letter from the pharmacy that she worked at:

D. Van Dijk Hillegersberg, October 1936

Certificate

Ms. Bé Oltmans has worked independently in my pharmacy for almost three years to my complete satisfaction. She works quickly and accurately, is diligent and dedicated. It is also great for an independent position.

Signed

D. Van Dijk

Batavia, 20 November

My darling Bebetje,

Tonight I am going to write early to you. Your last letters were so very cheerful, my wifey. That is, of course, because you see that time is really marching on. Don't you think that after all it goes fast? When I think about it, it seems a long time ago since you brought me to the train and we were making love to each other in the train to Utrecht. Oh, my angel, I will never forget that!! To be true, initially I had never been burdened by the thought of leaving Holland, but when it came to the point I felt so miserable about it and I did feel how we had absolutely grown together in that time: We truly belong to each other, my Bebetje. I believe we couldn't be without each other. I feel quite distinctly in the time that I am here now, even though we write each other so often, that I miss you, my dearest. That feeling will never go away. We must make our marriage so that it will be an example here in Indie. So many marriages go wrong here, even more than in Holland. But, my wifey, for us it will be beautiful together; we will make sure of that. One of the most important things here is to be and stay healthy, and I can stand the heat already quite well. A second factor is to get around with your salary. There are lots of people here who can't get around on 500 to 700 per month and are over their ears in debt. It is indeed very tempting here to spend, and the last few months I did spend more than in the beginning. But once you are here that won't happen anymore, and we will stay cosily at home together! When you are by yourself and you have so many friends, as I already have, there is always so much to do, and that always costs money. People are generally very free with their money and you can't stay away from them. You don't even have an excuse: "My wife is waiting for me with dinner."

I also got a membership for the swimming pool and swim every day. That's really nice, and we'll do that also when you are here. I think it is fl 10 per month for the two of us, rather expensive but cheaper than when you buy a ticket each time. Anyway, we'll see to it once you are here.

At the moment I don't know anything about your passage because Schlieper is away, but when he is back I will find out about it. I have no more news right now. Just remembered that it will be Nenne's birthday on Monday, so I will write him. You wrote that Kor is moving. Where is she going to live?

Many kisses and a big hug from your boy, Jaap.

Jaap's letter of November 20 is humorous. He has been away from his beloved Bé for seven months, and he is missing her very much. His recount of the train journey to Utrecht demonstrates that humans will be humans, even in 1936.

Bé has been busy, back in the Netherlands, navigating the paperwork required to get permission for the marriage. The wedding date is set for December 10, 1936. The Oltmans and Bebelaar families are busy with plans for the wedding day.

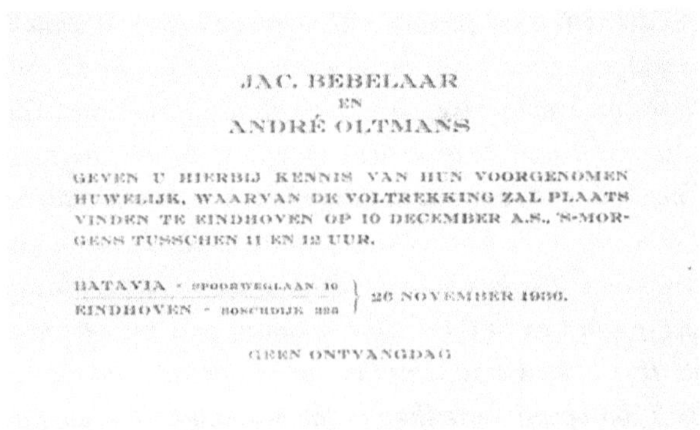

JAC. BEBELAAR
EN
ANDRÉ OLTMANS

GEVEN U HIERBIJ KENNIS VAN HUN VOORGENOMEN HUWELIJK, WAARVAN DE VOLTREKKING ZAL PLAATS VINDEN TE EINDHOVEN OP 10 DECEMBER A.S., 'S-MORGENS TUSSCHEN 11 EN 12 UUR.

BATAVIA - SPOORWEGLAAN 10
EINDHOVEN - BOSCHDIJK 388
26 NOVEMBER 1936.

GEEN ONTVANGDAG

This is the announcement card of the marriage between:

JAC. BEBELAAR
and
ANDRE OLTMANS

We hereby let you know that we will be
married on 10 December 1936

in Eindhoven in the morning between 11 and 12 o'clock.

BATAVIA - Spoorweglaan 10
EINDHOVEN - Boschdijk 326

26 November 1936

No reception

Eindhoven, 27 November 1936

My dearest boy,

What a lovely letter I got from you today my darling. I am always so very happy with it. Yesterday was a special day for us, you know. Did you think about it too? I found it a little disappointing that you did not write about our betrothal. I wrote you several times about it, but you did not react on it. Of course, you don't notice anything there, but do you realize that we are already in our "bridal days"? I am hereby including our betrothal announcement card. Do you like it? They were not too expensive. Yesterday I went with Anne to the city hall, not to be so alone. I had to answer all kinds of questions and put my signature in a very thick book. Then everything was recited and then it was over. When I got home the table was full of flowers, very nice, but I missed you very much my boy. Especially on a day like this, it is miserable not to be together. There were large bouquets of chrysanthemums from Mamma, Father, Kor, Hero, Nelle, and Bram. Further flowers from Anne and Herman and from Anne's parents, from your home a beautiful pot of begonias and from your little nieces a bouquet of tea roses. Nice, eh! Anne also made a beautiful breakfast linen. She is always so hearty. Kor also brought a beautiful cake, so it was altogether very festive. Those days pass for you almost unnoticed, but my thoughts are with you, darling. Today there were also flowers from the Goedharts. How short it was that we were engaged, eh Japie? Now that we get flowers and congratulations it looks as though it just happened. I will keep the letters so that you can also read them when I am in Indie. What a lovely time we are going to have Japie! I long very much for you, and we sure will be very happy together. Do you remember that you always used to say that we were an ideal couple? When you get this letter, then the next letter you will write you have to address to Mrs. Bebelaar because then we will be man and wife!!!

I hope that I soon will hear which boat I will go on; then I can start packing. When I go with the Indrapoera we couldn't have been later with our wedding day. I do want to go to Groeda for a few weeks. It will be quite busy with our wedding, because the Goedharts and the Pfeiffers will come, so it will be a house full of people. You will think a little about us on that day, so you will experience the wedding also in your thoughts.

This afternoon I went for my injections. I got them in my back. And although is was not unpleasant, I am a little stiff in my back, same as with you. Next week I have to go back to the doctor. Say, darling, I first had thought of sending you a St. Nicholas parcel but as we will be together shortly, and mailing is expensive, I decided not to; I hope you did not count on it. Nel did send something to Ber. I hope you are not too disappointed. How is it now with Ber? I find it such a miserable story. Nice that you took a swimming membership. It is a little expensive, but in Indie you have to do it. How nice it will be when I get you from the office and we go swimming. And it is also a lovely idea that we go home together and one of us does not have to leave again, because then we really belong together darling!

Next Sunday Nelle will come with Janneke, and yesterday Janneke was also here. That is such a little darling. You should see her: she is so sweet with her little nose. For that matter she is quite pretty looking. It will be nice if next year there will be another little one. I hope that Kor will be better off than the first time.

Lately it has been very cold here. We have to stoke quite hard to keep it warm. Right now, I am almost sitting on the stove to get warm; something you can't understand in your warm climate. But it is nice for you that it is a little cooler now in Batavia. How is it with Jo and Bert? Is she still ill? Today I sent a bag of sugared almonds to Gerrit. I first wanted to send some to other acquaintances as well, but in the end I didn't do it. It becomes so expensive. Regina sent me a long letter today. She now has a job at a notary who has an invalid child that needs special help. She is a teacher and now she has to teach the child and also care and nurse it. She likes the job a lot and sits with the family at the table for dinner. She has a lot of free time but has to be home in the evening. Egbert found the job inferior for her, so they had an argument and now they are no longer together. Regina wrote that if you couldn't agree on such a thing it was no true love, with which I agree. I found it a pity that they separated. They were just a nice couple.

Well my boy, I have not much more to tell you. Give my greetings to Jo and Bertand. Also, tell me more about Ber. Did the agent from Padang get the money from the people who left for Europe? What a story it was! Well my darling, my husband, in thought I give you many kisses and embrace you, from your bride,

Bé!

P.S. A letter with felicitations just came from the Pfeiffers. Bye darling

Batavia, 1 December 1936

My precious girl,

This will be the last letter I address to Miss Oltmans. The next one I will write to my own little wife. I find it almost like a dream. I get just so, without any ado, a little wife without noticing anything. It is really as if I fell asleep at night, dreamed that I was marrying, then woke up, and when I woke up and boom, it was true. My dearest Bebetje, I know for sure that we will be very happy together and stay that way. We will fight for it and under any circumstances help each other and together put our shoulders under it, even if it is hard and painful. My Bebetje, we will open our inner selves entirely up for each other. Understanding each other is the only thing that keeps our marriage good and permanent. We shouldn't be afraid to point at each other's errors or failures but try to correct them as best as we can. I am sure, my wifey, we can do that. We will make errors but will be strong enough to correct and overcome them. And so, improve ourselves. My own wife, don't be mad at me that I am just writing a short letter. I try to write you my deepest feelings. I think a lot about you and long for the time you are here, and I don't have to put my feelings on paper. I hope that it will be a day you'll keep in your dearest memories and that it always will stay undefiled in your heart. My dearest wife, that is the only wish from your own husband. Jaap

Batavia, 4 December 1936

My own wife,

This is the first letter you receive as Mrs. Bebelaar, Bebetje! You probably will find the change in name somewhat strange. My dear wife, I fervently hope that we will have an intensely happy marriage and that you never will find cause to doubt our marriage-happiness. We will do our best to keep our marriage pure and chaste. I am very proud of you, my Bebetje!

I just discovered something that I really regret. I forgot to send you flowers on the day of our betrothal. I wrote Mamma to order orchids for you. Those were always the flowers I really wanted to give you! I hope that you liked them when they came. Anyway, by the time you get this letter I will know because then we have talked together. I am enormously looking forward to the telephone conversation we have arranged. How lovely it will be to hear your voice, my darling. I really long for it! I am curious to know if they can keep it a secret until the moment you have to go to the telephone office! Mrs. Bebelaar goes to speak to her own husband, and I to my own wife!! My little wife, the dream becomes more and more a reality, and now it won't be long ere you are here yourself; how lovely that will be!

The cards you sent were nice. I have to figure out if I should place an ad in the paper here. I wonder if it is necessary. The people I know, already know it, and who else would be interested? It might *only be useful from a business point of view. Later you will hear about it.*

Say, girl, I thought to have written about our wedding day in a letter you must have received before November 26 or am I wrong, and did you get that letter much later? My dearest own wife, I do hope that our wedding day will be unforgettable for you and that together we will remember that day as the most important day in our life. The most beautiful day will be the day that you arrive here!!!

Well wifey, these days you are constantly in my thoughts and I also think a lot about the family. Please thank Mamma and Father for their nice letters. It is a pity that I did not write to them, but I hope that I can talk to them over the telephone.

Many warm kisses and a big hug in my thoughts from your own husband, Jaap

Jaap writes to Bé six days before their wedding day. He makes reference to a telephone call that they will have on their wedding day. He has arranged this as a surprise for Bé. On December 9, 1936, Bé receives notification that there will be a telephone call the next day with Jaap.

Mrs. Bebelaar - Oltmans Eindhoven 9 Dec 1936
Boschdijk 326
Eindhoven

Re: Your request for a telephone call with J. Bebelaar, Weltevreden, Batavia, Netherlands Indies.

Please be in the telephone cell of the Telegraph Office in Eindhoven on Thursday Dec. 10, 1936 at 14:10 pm.

Information:

If you can't make it let us know immediately.

In Neth. Indies there are cities that have special telephone cells where 4 persons can participate in the call.

Director
Eindhoven
9 Dec. 1936

On the Envelope: Please deliver and wait for answer.

RADIO-TELEFOONDIENST NEDERLAND/NEDERL.-INDIE

Aan ~~Mejuffrouw~~ Mevrouw ~~den Heer~~ Bebelaar - Oltmans
Boschdijk 326
te Eindhoven

Ingevolge ~~Uwe aanvrage dd.~~ ingekomen aanvrage van 9/12/1936 verzoek ik U voor het voeren van een telefoongesprek met

(naam en woonplaats van den aanvrager / ~~opgeroepene~~ in Ned.-Indie)

J Bebelaar Weltevreden

zich te vervoegen in de spreekcel van het telegraafkantoor
te: Eindhoven
den (datum) Donderdag 10/12 1936 te (uur) 14.10

Mocht U verhinderd zijn of geeft U er de voorkeur aan het gesprek van uit een andere spreekcel te voeren, dan gelieve U mij daarmede ten spoedigste in kennis te stellen.
Ten kantore worden inlichtingen verstrekt omtrent de plaatsen, waar voor den radiotelefoondienst met Ned.-Indië speciaal ingerichte spreekcellen zijn gevestigd, waarin voor vier personen gelegenheid bestaat aan het gesprek deel te nemen.

~~De Directeur,~~
De Kantoorhouder,

Dagteekeningstempel.
Ehv 9/12 36

The letters of congratulations start to flow in from family and friends.

Bilthoven, 9 December '36

Darling Andreije,

What do you think of the envelope with 'Mrs' written on it? I am sure this is the first one you received with this title. It seems so odd to address you like this, so strange. I am so terribly sorry I cannot congratulate you on this day in person like Father and Mother are doing, but it is just as well meant in writing.

I wish you lots of luck with a man like Jaap, and I wish the two of you many, many happy years together. You will be so happy once you are together in Batavia. When you see each other as man and wife and Jaap picks you up from the ship, we will think of you both.

I would love to come over for a week-end before you leave. I will hear from you if that is possible.

I will not be able to see all the presents; that is a shame. I am so glad that you like the table cloth and tea-cosy. It was a lot of work to make it. I am sure Jaap will like these, too. Make good use of these in your sunny Indische garden or patio. I wonder on what kind of table this will be used?

Thanks so much for your letter, Andre. Yes, we should not forget each other, of course, by writing each other. We should keep each other informed, for if we don't we will be even more apart. By writing each other regularly we will share all the joys, don't you think so, too?

You will now see your Father and Mother and everything around you with different eyes.

The coming last weeks will be very different now, but 2 ½ years is not that long I suppose. And you will have a wonderful new life ahead of you.

Dear child, I have no idea!

So, Andre, I wish you a lot of fun and strength today, girl.

Jaap will for sure think of you all day.

Goodbye, dear bride, and see you soon!

A big hug and many heartfelt greetings for your parents, Kor and Nel, your friend

Gerda Goedhart

Utrecht, 9 December 1936.

Dear Bé,

If this was one letter later I would have written Mrs Bebelaar instead of Miss Oltmans. From the bottom of my heart I would like to congratulate you and Jaap—happiness with this big step you are taking today, and I need not to add to this that I wish you a bright future with a lot of luck, also material luck but above all a spiritual luck. And for this future I hope for you especially that you, once you have arrived at the place where you end up so far away, that you will live as a couple that realize that: a good place in life, a happy marriage and good health are very special things in life. But that these things, and also the possible difficulties that may or may not be part of life are of greater value when you realize that our life is guided by a higher force. My excuses for preaching a little, but I mean this out of the depth of my heart. It is a big shame that for you this wedding day has lost a bit of its beauty, but within a month you will probably leave already or is this not known to you yet.

You know Wim Beukens, I think? He got married, too, and left for Indie yesterday and will be Health Officer. He will only know the place of assignment there on arrival. André, will you please congratulate your Mother and Father, too? Enjoy the time that is left for you here with them. This month I am in Utrecht together with Wim Kooistra (known to you, too) and have rented rooms here because I work together with Prof de Sno and that means I need to be available day and night.

To close this letter André, a beautiful day today and many more beautiful years in the future!

Best wishes, also for your parents from

Wim.

Their wedding day on December 10, 1936 was a special day for both of them. Individually, they each wrote to the other the next day.

Eindhoven, 11 December 1936

My dearest man,

What an enormous surprise you had for me yesterday, darling, I just didn't know what I saw and heard and so I will begin to tell you everything. In the morning when I was still dressing I was called downstairs and on the table was a beautiful bridal bouquet with pink carnations and white fresias and a lovely corsage of orchids, my favourite flower. You really have spoiled me with all this, my dear boy. A little later Uncle Paul and Aunt Ada came with Nel and father and mother. We had ordered a taxi and at 11 o'clock we went to the city hall. We had chosen a gratis wedding and although you are usually with three couples, this time we were alone. When we came, Mr.and Mrs.Goedhart were already waiting. Nice, eh! At 11.15 it started. First everything was rattled off, which made me laugh. But when we all had to put our signatures in the book and I clearly and with conviction had said, "I DO," it was over. The officer gave a nice little speech. I had the feeling that I was all alone and that your father was just a necessity. He started by saying, "Dear child ..." and then a speech which was very relevant to us, really beautiful, Japie. It was better than at the betrothal. And it was free. Nelle and Bram were married 2nd class but was not as nice as with us. Especially Mamma was very impressed, but they were all there. After it was finished everyone congratulated me and then we went home. In the car I put your wedding ring on my right hand. This is now a solid tie between us, and I hope and pray that we will be forever happy with each other.

At home there were a lot of presents from all our friends and family. You will have a lot to see when I am with you. At 2.10 came your telephone call. I found it fantastic that you had arranged that. At the phone office I had to wait 15 minutes, then a lady came and asked, "Mrs. Bebelaar?" In the cell I was all by myself because I wanted to be just with you. And it was so clear. How is it possible that we can talk while there is such a large distance between us! I can hardly understand. Your voice was very clear but sometimes a little creaky. Was it like that at your end, too? It was just delightful to hear your voice. Did you celebrate our wedding day with Jo and Bert? You probably did. I hope, my dear, that you felt the day to be a little different than usual. It definitely was for me, especially *with all your surprises. You always say that I shouldn't thank you, Japie, but this time I will still do it for all those nice things you prepared for me. In thought, I give you many kisses. We had our dinner at 5 o'clock because the people couldn't leave too late. Mamma had made a delicious dessert. We had 15 people at the table. Very cosy. At half past 8 they all left. Father and Mother went to Helmond where they would stay overnight with Aunt Kee. So today Dickie and I went to Helmond on our bike to say goodbye. Don't you think I am getting quite sportive? We bicycled along the Eindhovens Canal. Is it ever beautiful there. Do you remember that I waited for you there when you also came from Helmond? That is when we were just getting to know each other, although we already knew that we were meant for each other, and now we are married. Fine Japie! I am really proud of my man.*

Yesterday there were more telegrams, 11 altogether and also congratulating letters. I will send all of it by boat mail, then you can also read them later. Dickie will go home tomorrow. He didn't get the job at Philips. What a pity for him.

I was disappointed yesterday when you said in our telephone talk, that I wouldn't be on the boat in January. So, we may have to wait a few more months. It's a pity, but we will survive even if I very much long for you. At least we are married now, so that is something we have achieved! Well my darling, I have nothing more to tell you. Your letter of today didn't arrive yet, possibly tomorrow. This is the first letter I write to you as your own wife. Strange, eh? But it is really true. I give you many big kisses and a big hug from your wifey,Bé.

Bé was so happy that they were married. Her astonishment about the ability to speak on a phone with such a great distance between them is childlike. How can something so inconceivable, be possible?

Batavia, 11 December 1936

My own dearest wife,

Don't look at my strange handwriting, I still have to get used to the wedding ring. A strange feeling. I was very happy that I could hear your voice. How amazing that we could be so far away from each other and yet could talk to each other on our wedding day. It did me a lot of good, only it was a pity that I had to tell you that your passage had been delayed. I couldn't explain it any further and I also can't harp on it with Schlieper. He is satisfied with me and you know: "Business goes before the girl." I also have to make sure that they are satisfied with my work. So, also the office manager Mr. Schneider treats me as a colleague and comes to discuss items in a pleasant way. The general office mood here is quite friendly and so it is pleasant to work here. They do demand a lot from you and you have to be ready day or night, but then again there are few firms that pay as well as this one. Bebetje, you will see that with this firm we really have hit the jackpot. Make the best of the few months you have to stay with Mamma and Father. You will see that time will fly. I think a lot about you, my wife!

I will now stop with many big kisses and a big hug, your Jaap

P.S. What beautiful flowers you sent. There were also some from Jo and Bert, Tine v.d. Meyde and the girls from home. It was like a flower shop when I got home.

What a year 1936 was for Bé and Jaap. Between April and December Jaap trained in Germany for a new job, left a few weeks later for the Dutch East Indies, arrived there and got settled. Bé took on the responsibility of arranging for their wedding and ending the busy year with a wedding ceremony on December 10. Their plans to be reunited have been delayed. Bé resigned her position at the pharmacy in October, anticipating that she would be departing to join Jaap in Batavia soon after their wedding.

1937

Newly married, Bé and Jaap long to be together again. Good news comes that Bé has been booked to travel aboard the M.S. *Johan van Oldenbarnevelt*, departing from Amsterdam on February 24, 1937 with a scheduled arrival in Batavia on March 25, 1937. The ship will take the route of Amsterdam to Southampton (England), Genoa (Italy),

Port Said (Egypt), Aden (Yemen), Colombo (Sri Lanka), Sabang (N. Sumatra), Belawan (Sumatra), Batavia (Java).

Delpher

J Bebelaar

De Sumatra post

Passagiers van het m. s. Johan van Oldebarnevelt, d.d. 24 Februari van Amsterdam naar Batavia vertrokken, en 22 Maart te Belawan-Deli verwacht.:

Z. H. Pangeran Adipati Ario Mangkoe Nagoro VII., G. K. Ratoe Timoer., G. Raden Adjeng Siti Noeroel Koesoemowardhani., Tengkoe Kamil., Tengkoe Mansoersjah., fam. Mr. G. H. Aeyelts., Raden Ajoe Soejoedono., B. Alberts., mevr. A. Allen., fam. J. Alt en 2 kinderen., fam. J. Andriesse en kind., Dr. R. P. Bachlin., A. Baks., fam. A.E. Banse., A. A. Banse. fam. Mr. W. F. C. J. Baukema., mej. H. W. Bäumer., fam. Ir. A. J. Beauchez en 2 kinderen., mevr. A. P. J. Bebelaar., mevr. J. M. Beezemeer., J. A. van der Bent., fam. A. van Benthem en dochter., fam. H. E. G. Berkhoff., H. J. Beumer., fam. J.

De post

NAAR INDIE

Passenger List for the *Johan van Oldenbarnevelt*

Captain: M. F. Mörzer Brunns

Passangers from the Johan van Oldenbarnevelt left 24 February 1937 from Amsterdam left near Batavia and is expected 22 March 1937 at Belawan-Deli: Z. H. Pangeran Adipati Ario Mangkoe Nagoro VII, G. K. Ratoe Timoer, G. Raden Adjeng Siti Noeroel Koesoemowardhani, Tengkoe Kamil, Tengkoe Mansoersjah, fam. Mr. G. H. Aeyelts, Raden

Ajoe Soejoedono, B. Alberts, Mrs. A. Allen, fam. J. Alt and 2 children, fam. J. Andriesse and child, Dr. R. P. Bachlin, A. Baks, fam. A. E. Banse, A. A. Banse, fam. Mr. W. F. C. J. Baukema, Miss H. W. Bauner, fam. Engineer A. J. Beauchez and 2 children, Mrs. **A. P. J. Bebelaar**, Mrs. J. M. Beezemer, J. A. van der Bent, fam. A. van Benthem and daughter, fam. H. E. G. Berkhoff, H. J. Beumer, fam. J. R. Beute and child, Mrs. J. J. Bianchi and child, fam. D. Biersteker and child, F. M. Billroth, fam. J. H. Bitters and child, D. S. Bloamendaal, Miss E. M. Blijdenstein, Miss. C. M. de Boer, Miss P. J. W. de Boer, fam. H. W. H. van den Bogaard, Mrs. H. M. J. Boon, A. Bos, P. Bos, A. L. van den Bosch, fam. A. F. Bosman and child, Miss W. F. Bötterman, G. Bouma, Mrs. M. J. van Boxtel, fam. W. E. J. Boysen and child, H. van den Brink, Mrs. E. A. Broekhoff and child, Lady A. W. S. von Brzeska, D. Bijl, Mrs. B. Combier and 3 children, Colonel The Hon. E. Coke, N. Commijs, W. H. Cotton, Mrs. M. Cupido, fam. M. van Dalm and 2 children, fam. W. P. van Dam and 6 children, Mrs. D. Darphorn and 2 children, J. Deeken, Mrs. Mrs. W. C. Denninghof Stelling and 2 children, L. M. Diks, fam. J. W. Dimonti, Mrs. J. Doezie and child, Dr. E. F. Drion, fam. K. Drost and 2 children, Miss A. A. Drijver, Miss. B. K. Drijver and 2 children, H. F. Den Dulk and child, Mrs. A. van Dijk and child, fam. M. Dijkstra, fam. G. van Ee, A. Elhorst, J. B. A. van den Elshoudt and child, J. Ch. Emmels, Ds. I. H. F. S. Enklaar, A. J. Enneman and child, G. P. L'Estrange, fam. E. A. van Eyden and 3 children, Mrs. W. A. Eykhoudt and child, fam. B. H. Farret Jentink, fam. Engineer J. Feikema and 2 children, Th. Fels, F. Fleischer, fam. J. J. Furstner, Mrs. E. Fuyt and 2 children, Mrs. J. A. J. Gallas and child, J. A. Geers and 2 children, Mrs. Geers and 2 children, Mrs. A. C. Gentis and child, fam. Dr. J. H. A. Gerlach, H. H. M. Gerrits, fam. W. P. Gilliam and 5 children, Mrs. A. W. Gladpootjes and child, J. H. Goldberg, Miss. G. Gort, fam. J. de Graaf and child, fam. J. D. Graham, fam. Engineer J. Gramberg, Mrs. C. Groen, Eningeer. A. Guillon, G. M. Haars, Mrs. C. Hage, Mrs. A. C. Hannessen, F. M. Hasselman, fam. Mr. J. G. Hazeloop and child, N. M. J. van Hees, fam. P. van den Herik and 3 children, fam. J. Hermans, W. van der Heul, P. Den Heyer, Mrs. L M. H. Heymans and child, W. E. CH. Heymans and child, A. van Heyningen, Lord W. F. Hillebrandt, J. F. van Hillegondsberg, H. W. Hintzbergen. Engineer H. van der Hoeven, J. A. van den Hof, F. Hoff.

fam. A. F. Holm, H. L. C. de Hoog, W. J. H. Houbolt, A. van Houten, L. H. Huizenga, J. van Hulsbergen, J. J. Hundscheidt, G. Huntley, Miss A. Huysmans, Miss A. A. Iken, fam. J. de Jager and 2 children, P. J. van der Jagt, Mrs. A. V. Jahhn, Miss E. C. Jahn, Mrs. J. Janisch and child, H. H. M. Jansen, P. Jansen, D. de Jong, Miss A. W. de Jonge van der Halen, Mrs. P. A. Jongenschap and 2 children, fam. W. Joziasse, H. M. Julsing, fam. G. W. Kalsbeek and 5 children, Miss A. E. Kaper, fam. Engineer G. Kappelle, fam. H. Kaufmann, E. Keasberry Jr. and son, fam. A. Keller, fam. J. Kerkhof and son, Mrs. G. G. Kern, J. Kers, fam. A. E. Ketelaar and 2 children, W. Keyzer, Mrs. F. H. King and child, Mrs. J. Kitovitz, fam. Engineer E. Klaij and child, B. H. Klein Kormelink, G. Klepper, Mrs. M. H. A. de Klerk and 2 children, J. H. H. Knies, K. K. Knies, Mrs. E. Knijpenga, Th. M. A. H. Kockelkoren, C. J. de Koning, W. Koningstein, fam. T. Koopmans, fam. Mr. J. V. M. van Koot, fam. H. J. K. Kooyman, J. Kos, Ds. K. Kostelijk, J. Kosten, Mrs. W. Koudstaal. fam. C. J. M. Kramers, A. W. van Krieken, Zeereew. Pater B. H. A. ten Kroode, Mrs. H. M. A. Kruk and child, fam. J. H. Kubinek and child, W. A. Kuyck, Mrs. D. Last and 2 children, fam. F. van Leeuwen and child, Mrs. L. F. Lerway Day, fam. Engineer Lie Tjiong Hian, fam. J. P. Linck and 2 children, Th. M. van Lint, Mrs. E. R. J. List and 2 children, Lo Kwang Pheng, Miss E. A. Logher, Mrs. A. J. Loos and child, fam. N. van de Loosdrecht and 2 children, F. A. Lücking, Miss C. Luiting. Fam. S. Makkinga and child, Dr. K. Markovits, Mrs. A. J. Marquart, Mrs. E. Maurer, Engineer K. F. Meertens, Engineer G. Meesters, Mrs. T. H. Meursing, Mrs. M. P. von Meijenfeldt and 3 children, fam. Ds. H. G. Meynen, Zeereerw. Mere Michaele, fam. A. Monster and 2 children, F. Morris, R. Naarding, fam. G. Nachtegaal, fam. J. W. F. Nanlohy and 5 children, fam. W. Nanning, R. M. Noto Soeroto, C. B. Oomens, H. van Oostrum, fam. W. E. Palstra, Mrs. N. E. Pankhurst, P. Peereboom, W. F. Pennenburg, H. M. van Peperstraten, A. Peters, A. Peters, Miss M. M. J. Petit, fam. L. B. Peuschgens and child, W. H. Polet and 3 children, Mrs. J. M. J. Postuma, fam. C. F. Pow, fam. H. A. Preuyt, A. J Quak. Fam. A. A. G. de Raadt and 3 children, J. Rademaker, fam. P. A. Reuvekamp and 3 children, Mrs. S. Reyers and 2 children, J. H. Reynaud, C. de Ridder, Miss M. L. Robbers, fam. C. C. M. van Romondt and child, E. Ronlez. Mrs. G. van Rooyen and 3 children, Engineer N.

J. van Rossum and 2 children, fam. G. J. de Ruiter and 2 children, B. B. M. Rupert, Mrs. T. W. Rutten, Mrs. M. C. de Rijk, J. Scheffer, fam. Scheltema, W. Schilthuizen, **W. Schlieper**, B. J. Schlögl, H. J. Schlömer, Mrs. R. A. Scholten, J. A. Schuller and child, fam. K. L. Schüller, fam. N. H. A. J. Schulte and 2 children, fam. K. Seeuwen and child, fam. G. L. J. De Senerpont Domis and child, fam. J. Slijkhuis,Miss A. H G. Smeding, Miss H. Smid, H. J. J. Smit, fam.W. K. Soeters, Mrs. A. B. G. Spangenberg, Mrs. L. Sprandel, L. J. W. Spijker, Mrs. O. H. Stam and child, Mr. H.R. Stieltjes and 2 children, J. Stolp, Mrs. W. van Straaten and child, fam. J. Straub and 3 children. Mrs. J. Stubert and child, fam. E. Tanis and child, H. Teeuwissen, Mrs. C. Terhaar and 2 children, fam. S.Terwey and child, Miss Terwey, Dr. A. A. Thiadens, J. Thiebout, fam. P. G. Tdeman, Eerw. Zuster Valentine, W. C. P. van der Veer, J. A. A. L. in 't Veld; J. van de Velde, fam. Ds. J. J. Verdenius and 2 children, Mrs. J. A. L. Verdier, J. A. W. Verhoeff, G. Verhoog, Engineer W. Ch. A. Vink, A. Visbeek, Mrs. H. Visscher, M. C. van Vlierden, P. Vonders, Mrs. C. J. Voogt and child, C. G. J. Voorham; Mrs. J. Voute, fam. F. Vreede, fam. Engineer A. L. de Vries and 2 children, A. Th. Vromen, B. D. G. Wardenburg, Prof. Dr. A. Widmaier, H. F. Willemse, L. J. A. Wit, fam. A. Wolfrat and 2 children, Mrs. J. H. P. Wurfbain and 2 children, fam. J. Wijfje, fam. G. Ch. P. Wijnands, J. P. Wijnands, Mrs. A. S. Wijsman and child, J. B. F. Yates.

(Source: «Gevonden Op Delpher - De Sumatra Post.» Delpher.nl. Accessed August 19, 2018. https://www.delpher.nl/nl/kranten/view?query=J. Bebelaar&facets[periode][]=2|20e_eeuw|1930-1939|1937|&page=1&coll=ddd&identifier=ddd:010383743:mpeg21:a0181&resultsidentifier=ddd:010383743:mpeg21:a0181.)

Batavia, 12 March 1937

My dearest own wife,

A hearty welcome now that you have arrived in Indies first port, Sabang. I hope that we will have many happy years here together, in true married happiness and that together we can build a real satisfying career here. You will soon notice that the wife here can cooperate more with the career of her husband than in Holland. But you are the wife for me, and we sure will succeed!! We already said so many times that we are an ideal couple! And that is for sure!

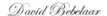

When I got your last letter from Holland this afternoon I was so sorry that I had not written to you in Genoa and Port Said, but I hadn't because I thought that we would soon see each other anyway so better could tell what we had experienced. It sounds unbelievable, eh? After this I don't write any more.

Dear wife, when you arrive here you should have one suitcase with enough clothing and things for 5 days. The rest of the luggage will be taken care of by Mr. Bookelaar, the clerk from the firm. You will only have to tell them on board that all your luggage and your trunk will be taken care of by the Schlieper firm. In the afternoon we go directly to Selabintana. Max will drive us in his own car to Weltevreden (suburb of Batavia) so he will only take your suitcase. You also shouldn't wear a big hat because you would have to hang on to it underway. I couldn't rent our home until April 1st because his departure has been postponed a month. So, the first month we will live in a hotel from where we can quietly arrange everything for the house.

Well my dearest wife, you know most of it now. Schlieper debarks in Medan, but Schlomer stays on board until here. I hope you have had a nice voyage and that you could still amuse yourself on the last part. Give my greetings to my "bosses" when you see them. Isn't Schlomer a nice guy? Many warm kisses and a real big hug from your longing Jaap.

Selabintana Resort, Sukambumi, Java

Bé's first introduction to her upcoming life in the Dutch East Indies, was interesting. Bé's niece, Janneke, told me the following story: Jaap and Bé went to the Selabintana Resort for their wedding night. We can assume they had dinner and a warm reuniting. The next morning, they woke up and everything in their room was gone, including the clothes they wore to bed that night. As the story was told, someone had sprayed a dust into the room which rendered them unconscious, and they then proceeded to enter the room and take all the belongings the couple had with them, down to the underwear they wore to bed. Welcome to your new life.

1938

There are no communications found from 1937 or 1938. It has been determined that Jaap has been successful in his role with his employer and has been transferred to the Medan, Sumatra office to replace the manager, who is being relocated to Surabaya. Jaap and Bé make the move to Medan late 1938 or early 1939.

1939

Taking on his new responsibilities at the office in Medan, Jaap also takes on an extra role. The manager he is replacing was on a council that lobbies to help citizens who are victims of high rates in commercial lending. This commission fights usery in lending and works to establish policy for the elimination of this practice. The following is an article from the Sumatra Post, February 24, 1939:

Anti-loan-gouging in the past year

A report about the creation of the new legislation.

Mr. J. Reparon, honorary member

During the annual general meeting (AGM) of the association of anti-loan-gouging held last night at Hotel De Boer, the chairman, Mr. Ch.E.E. Kuntze regrettably had to note that there was no interest from any of the association members to hold the AGM. The association needs the full support of its members, which is why the chairman is considering to make the AGM a more open meeting going forward and introduce brief lectures about relevant topics like, the recently created legislation around anti-loan-gouging. Following this Mr. Kuntze indicated that he as chairman (which position he took as of yesterday) of the association is intending to do much about the loan-gouging, as he believes this is highly important as this is one of the worst parts of Indonesian society.

Report from the chairman of the committee.

Next, the chairman of the committee, Ms. S. Blankenstein, provided her report from which the following is extracted: The board made a couple of changes in 1938. In August

1938 the chairman, Mr. G. Pitlo resigned. He had held that position for 4 years in which the association grew significantly and had become a strong association. "We will remember him for his character", said the chairman of the committee. Mr. C.E.E. Kuntze, was willing to take on the role of chairman. Mr. F.J. Bruggeman was succeeded by Mr. C. Bakker, Mr. de Rooy was succeeded by Mr. Bergsma. The committee added Mr. J. Woudsma. The secretary treasurer, Mr. J. Reparon, had to resign from his duties as a result of relocation. He worked for the association since its inception. He will be missed, as, for years, he was the person that always came up with new initiatives, and his work for the association was near and dear to his heart.

As a result, a marketing campaign was run that can be seen as an example for all associations of anti-loan-gouging in Indonesia. I would like to thank him for everything he has done for us. We will miss him, but we are convinced that in his new residency of Soerabaja, he will once again be a string voice for the anti-loan-gouging work done on Java. Mr. Woude has been found willing to take on the role of secretary and **Mr. J. Bebelaar** the role of treasurer.

The legislation that had been long awaited, the 1936 lLending ordinance, finally came about. The funding agreement came into force on January 1, 1938 and applies to all provinces on Java and on the east coast of Sumatra. The fact that the declaration of applicability is limited to the east coast shows that, according to the government's view, the loan-gouging has become a real problem of large proportion here. The great work of the association has certainly contributed to the government's understanding of thc problem. As a result of this ordinance a lender can only lend money if they have obtained a license. This will ensure that the lending of money is done in a good way.

The new anti-loan-gouging ordinance protects the victims in a much better way than in the ordinance from 1916. The work of the association will be facilitated by this new ordinance that facilitates the fact that measures can be easily taken against perpetrators and information and advice can be provided. On the other hand, the ability to intervene will make work more important and useful. In most cases that were discovered, mediation resulted in a satisfactory outcome. The cooperation of the VolkskredietBank has greatly contributed to this cause.

"Our insights into anti-loan-gouging have changed over the years. At first, our struggle was characterized by a fierce attitude towards the perpetrating lenders and a not always properly characterized pity for the victims. Slowly we have come to a clearer insight. We are convinced that, on the one hand, there are lenders that, provided that they are guided properly, fulfill an economic need, and that on the other hand there are many so-called victims who have low wages and each time lend more money, knowing full well that they will not be able to fulfill their obligations in the end, who going forward can not count on our support and assistance anymore. This way we have increasingly positioned ourselves in a mediating role that has yielded great results."

Mr Reparon took the floor and thanked Mr Blankestein for his praise, noting that he was not aware that he had provided such praiseworthy work. "I have only done my duty, and the praise is certainly exaggerated". My successor will surely do the job as well, or better, however I will regard the past couple of years as the most beautiful in my life. I will miss the association and the meetings but will continue to live and breathe the work of the anti-loan-gouging association. Finally, I thank Mr Reparon for the confidence he had in him.

The Annual Reports of the Secretary

In the Secretary's annual report over the year's 1938, Mr. J. Reparon states, among other things, the following: My thoughts go back to 1931 when I met Mr. Schoorl, Mr. Gooszen, Mr. Trouw and Mr. Van De Bergh, and we started the anti-loan-gouging work. We knew that it would be a difficult and long-lasting battle. However, I am happy to have experienced the birth of the anti-loan-gouging ordinance. The perpetrators of this loan-gouging have been reigned in more than ever before and most certainly our association will be a force to be reckoned with in the future, more so than ever before. That our association received a lot of support is evidenced by the fact that we started with 18 members, but throughout our existence, we had 400 members. Now at the end of 1938 we have 200 members. The departing members left us as a result of relocation. From something so small, grew something very formidable. How interesting were our committee meetings and what a love for the work all committee members have shown. When I tally up all the results of the past years, I ask myself the following question, "May I be satisfied with what we have achieved?" Then I will not give an answer to this myself, but the future will let us know whether our goal was worth it. I have good memories of the first 4 years, when we did not have our own office, and every free hour we had was spent on our cause, the anti-loan-gauging. And how happy we were if we could recruit 25 or more new members through our campaigns. I also think back of the amount of victims that we could not save from the loan-gougers hands. We did not have the illusion that our cause would sometimes not be temporary, and that some victims would again fall in the hands of perpetrators. We have often been angry when we could not help a case due to the lack of legislation or lack of evidence. We were also surprised at times that a victim would have entrusted us with their case, we managed to help them, but later we found that they had other debt that they had not informed us about and failed to fulfill their obligations. Several times, scammers have misused our assistance as well. Those who had borrowed twenty times (or more) of their monthly salary and had used this money for useless purposes, knowing full well that they could never meet their repayment obligations. These kinds of people were unconditionally left to their own fate.

We do not want to end our report before once again calling on the employers' cooperation. Let them remember that an employee who is in the hands of the loan-gougers, is not a full and productive employee. We impress upon employers to conduct a survey among your employees and guarantee you that you will find that a large part of your staff has borrowed money from a loan-shark. Give the person in question another chance. Call for us and surprise our association with a donation.

With the further support of our members and the government, and with our current board, I have full confidence in the future of the anti-loan-gouging association.

The work process

The work process of the association can be reported on as follows: Just like in recent years, we succeeded in requesting the help of the Volkskredietbank multiple times, allowing us to effectively restructure the debt of the victims. In 1938, the Volkskredietbank provided loans to victims for an amount of $1,825 (1937, $2,977). The desire over the past few years to get a higher line of credit by putting up a $500 deposit was however not realized. It turned out that when a victim has no full collateral coverage, The Volkskredietbank can not provide a line of credit unless we fully guaranteed it. It should be clear that we can not take on this risk. Nevertheless, we will continue to focus on this issue and we hope to find another solution in the future. The work of our office does not change.

The administrator of our association will make every effort to reach an agreement with the lender in favor of the victims. However, here we occasionally encountered that victims, once an agreement was reached on a repayment scheme where the victim paid a reasonable amount on a monthly basis related to the monthly salary, did not comply with the agreement and repayment schedule. What do we do in those circumstances? We could not notify the victim’s employer as they asked us not to do so, which left us powerlessness. It was much easier for us to deal with the matters which were brought to us by employers who had reviewed their personnel files and found victims that they obliged to work with us. In these cases, we have a clear mandate. In 1938, we still considered sending the victims an invoice for the services that we provided defending their interests. On Java, almost all anti-loan-gouging associations do this. Batavia has almost no other income, but the general opinion was that we would lose the strength and sympathy of our donors if we charged our clients. We prefer to raise money by calling out to the socially-responsible population for donations occasionally.

The number of cases handled in 1938 was:

Europeans	17
Chinese	11
Inlanders	93
	121

In 1938 only 1 legal action made it to the courts. As previously reported, this was because all cases could generally be negotiated and settled between the lender and the borrower.

Furthermore, as in previous years, many payment arrangements were made through our office. In 1938, $6300 of payment arrangements were negotiated by our association.

Annual Report of the Treasurer

In the treasurer's annual report, we note the following:

Net revenue over the past year was around $400 less than in 1937. However, the contributions increased by $974.50 to $1018.25. Largely as a result of not receiving any government contributions, the total went down strongly.

The fact that we did not receive government contributions this time was because the government has decided to distribute their contributions in all reasonableness and honesty over many of the anti-loan-gouging associations. Irrespective of which method is followed, the Medan association can expect a larger share than it had previously received, being 6% of the total contribution. Fortunately, we were able to balance the books even without this government support in 1938. Nevertheless, we should not forget that we can not expect the administrator will work for us for a very small salary indefinitely. In future, we therefore have to expect larger expenses. Expenses in 1938 remained virtually equal to 1937, being $2097 and $2034 respectively. The loss over 1938 was $19.97, which was deducted from the associations equity, which was $1450.83 at the end of the year. Membership fell sharply from 230 to 196. Fortunately, no one canceled their membership, but this decline was attributable to relocations and repatriations, and the fact that no major marketing campaign took place in 1938. In 1939 we will launch a major marketing campaign.

At the point of "board member election" (the new composition has already been reported in the staff changes), the chairman once again thanked Mr. Reparon for the work he had done over the past few years, after which Mr Kuntze proposed that the departing secretary treasurer would be awarded the highest honor in the association, being the appointment of honorary member. This proposal was widely accepted by a loud applause. The Q&A round did not add anything further, after which the meeting was adjourned.

The 1940s: A Decade of Family Growth and Crisis

1940

Jaap and Bé welcome 1940 with much anticipation. Professionally, Japp is excelling at work and is very involved with the committee work. Personally, Jaap and Bé are anxiously anticipating the arrival of their first child. These are exciting times for the family.

On April 28, 1940, in Medan, Sumatra, at the St. Elizabeth hospital, Jaap and Bé become the proud parents of Wouter Jan: a son to carry on the family name.

De Heer en Mevrouw
J. BEBELAAR - Oltmans
geven met groote blijdschap kennis van de geboorte van hun zoon
WOUTER JAN
St. Elisabeth Ziekenhuis
Heemskerklaan 18, Medan 28 April 1940

St. Elizabeth Ziekenhuis – Medan, Sumatra, 1940

Soon after the birth, Jaap makes phone calls back to the Netherlands to tell the family the good news.

Bennekom, 28-4-1940

Dear Jaap

Congratulations Jaap and we hope still many happy years together with wife and kid. You are now celebrating your birthday as a father of a son, with whom you must be very happy. You will not know how happy we were with this morning's telegram and especially when we heard that everything is fine.

The last few days we were very much anxious and hardly dared to go out. We called your Dad right away but got no answer. We will try again tomorrow at 8.30 am. We wish you lots of luck with your newborn boy and hope that he is going to be a nice boy. You must be happy as well, now that it has all past, and it must have been a trying time for you as well, especially when the baby was overdue. I hope, Jaap, that you will write us soon about how everything went. You do understand that we think of lot about you.

Many regards, and I hope that Bé will be home soon with her little son.

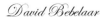

Affectionately, your Mom.

Dear Bé and Jaap,

It was quite a relief when we received the telegram; it did take quite a bit of patience from our side.

And now, many congratulations to the two of you with your boy, and I hope that he will grow up in good health and as a good and valuable member of society and that with whom you will be with.

And I do wish that Bé will recover soon and that you will be home soon.

How did you get that nice name? Jan is very common and likely will refer to me, but Wouter—where did you get that from? I have, as far as I know, never heard the name "Wouter van Jaap" in my family.

However, it is a real Dutch name.

And, Jaap, now I take this opportunity to congratulate you on your birthday. I do hope that you will celebrate this many times in the future, in good health with your wife and son. And, of course, I congratulate Bé and Wouter on your birthday. At the time you receive this letter we should have a letter from Jaap about how it is with you all. We do look forward to that news. Although it might be a bit early, Jaap, I do believe that you never had such a nice present as this little guy from Bé.

Dear Guys, be good, and kind regards and a firm handshake for Jaap, a big kiss for Bé and a gentle little kiss for the little Wouter, from Dad and Opa

Bé's parents are happy to hear of the birth of Wouter Jan. They were getting anxious as the birth had gone past the expected due date.

Bennekom, April 28, 1940

Dear Bé,

Today at 12 o'clock we got the news from Arnhem by telegram.

How happy we are, Bé, especially because everything is fine, dear. I wish you all the best with your little son and a speedy recovery from the delivery. And then, even a Sunday-child!! If we could only be with you for a moment. But in my thoughts, I often see you and then it is just as if I am talking with you.

We think that you chose a beautiful name and father is proud that he also is called Jan. Is Wouter a name in Jaap's family, or do you just like the name? I am looking forward to a letter from Jaap. Does the baby look like one of you? The post was very considerate to forward the telegram because the post-office here is closed on Sundays.

I hope that you will soon be home again with your baby, Bé. I also congratulate you on Jaap's birthday and wish you both many happy years together. If everything is right, this letter should just arrive on his birthday, which you can celebrate with the three of you! Maybe you will already be home by then. Myself, I am luckily all right. Groot drives an army truck: 5 hours on and 5 hours off.

Bé, all the best with you. We are very proud that we now have a grandson, and you my child, are now a little mother!

Warm kisses from your mother, and also give my grandson a little kiss from his Granny.

Letters from Bé's sisters, Nel and Kor follow:

Groede, April 29, 1940

Dear Bebel and Jaap

Sincere congratulations with your son. It must be a relief now that the baby is born. Bé, you must be happy and maybe you might be home now for Jaap's birthday anniversary—the three of you. Jaap, many happy returns on your birthday. Your first one as a Dad. You are getting old, are you not? But with kids it is not bad to get older. They do give you quite a few worries but a lot more joy. It was good to hear that my parcel arrived. I do hope that he is going to have a lot of fun with it. When you are back home and settle in, then you should write Han a letter and tell him how things went and if you feed him yourself, etc.

For now, bye dear boy and together enjoy your first new born.

With our best regards from all of us, and for the three of you a big kiss from
Nel

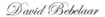

Eindhoven, April 29, 1940

Dear Bé and Jaap,

We congratulate you warmly on the birth of Wouter Jan and at the same time on Jaap's birthday. That is then your first birthday celebration with the three of you. Bé can just be on the mend, at least if she is recovering quickly. I never was quick and stayed in bed for 2 weeks. It is not a small thing to bring such a small creature into the world. Even though the doctors say that it is quite normal. How did it go Bé? Was the baby in a good position? Tell us what he weighed and is he drinking all right? And please send us a picture if you can. Such small babies are usually not very photogenic, but I would love to see it. You will see Bé, when you can walk again, how light it is now that you don't have to carry it anymore, you will with less than before; at least that was the case with me.

With those last exciting days (general mobilization because of the German threat) we went to The Hague. Herre stayed in Eindhoven; he was head of the people who had to alarm all kinds of people of the danger. We (I and the kids) were picked up at 4 in the morning to go to the train that took us to The Hague. We left with the first train; there were only 4 trains that day. At first, we stayed with Herre's family but later found a boarding house near Scheveningen. The kids didn't understand what was happening, first the train unexpectedly and then a strange place to stay. But they especially enjoyed playing on the beach in Scheveningen. Everything is fine with the kids; they have a lot of fun.

Oh, do you remember that on June 15, it is Father and Mother's 35th wedding anniversary? Will we do something together, or do you have any plans, Bé? We cannot let it go unnoticed. Let us know what you think.

Well guys, give the little Wouter Jan a warm kiss from us. He is a Sunday child, just like Janneke. They say Sunday children have a long life. Who knows?

All the best with you, Bé! Many hearty greetings and love from all of us.

Your Herre and Kor

The first letter arrives from the Bebelaar family: a letter from Jaap's brother Nico and his wife Frans.

Rotterdam, May 1, 1940

Dear Jaap and Be,

And again, the Bebelaar family has been enriched with the birth of a son and heir. What a family! Just immortal! Okay, let me start to sincerely congratulate the happy Dad and the yet happier Mom, and I hope that that he is going to be a big, real, healthy Dutch lad, who will bring you much happiness and pleasure. And if you are lucky the pleasure will start soon. You will not believe it, but our Ronny started to cheer from pleasure when he heard the news that he had a little cousin.

Is everything going all right? And Bé as well? All right, we will have to be patient until we get the latest news from you. Frans is, of course, very curious, and so am I. A boy, what luck, on the same day that our Ronny was baptized in the Prinzen church by Rev Stam: a day which has meaning as well.

I will have to leave some space for Frans, who wants to add some more. Therefore, I am going to end here, but not before I have congratulated Jaap on his birthday, as well as Bé and little Wout, and I hope it is going to be a pleasant day. I will end with the best regards to you.

Nic

Dear Jaap and Be,

Hurrah, another boy. Yes, it is great, but first of all congratulations and as well on Jaap's birthday. He must be proud now that he is a Dad. That is nice and a Sunday child, everything went all right? We are very curious, of course, but take it easy.

It is so pleasant in the house. The weather is beautiful now, and we can often go outside with him, or otherwise he stands in my mother's garden.

You know, next month we are going to move to the ground floor of a house two houses down the road from here. We are looking forward to it, as well as for Ronny. Ronny is getting so smart and wants to play and grasp everything. He is allowed more fruit juices and porridge in the evening; that is so funny.

When we are living on the ground floor he can be outside more frequently. There is an extra room, which we can make into a nice baby room. For the time being he is going to stay in our room, which is quite big, but when Ronny gets a bit older we want him to have his own room.

We did receive your letter in which you wrote that you received the package. Yes, I still make nice little things and now that the weather is nice he does not have to be dressed that warm because he is very healthy and strong. Bé, I wish you and your son all the best and hope to hear from you. I will end with the best wishes and kind regards and from Ronny and a little parcel for Wouter and you two.

Frans.

The next letter to arrive is from Jaap's employer:

J. C. SCHLIEPER

BATAVIA-CENTRE, May 3, 1940

Dear Mr. Bebelaar,

Being grateful to have received the news of the birth of your son, I do congratulate you on the occasion.

With kind regards and best wishes for the health of mother and child,

Sincerely J.C. Schlieper

Wouter held by nurse/nun at hospital, and Bé with Wouter as they prepare to go home for the first time.

Arriving home at Heemskerklaan 18, Medan, Sumatra

Bé, Wouter and Jaap are now a happy family, all under one roof. Their life ahead of them looks exciting and full of hope. But, news from the Netherlands changes everything on May 10, 1940. Germany has invaded the Netherlands as part of its conquest in World War II.

There is a concern for members of the Oltmans and Bebelaar families across the Netherlands, in Rotterdam, Bennekom, Eindhoven and Groede.

The ramifications of Germany's action in the Dutch homeland are felt in The Dutch East Indies (DEI). As a territory of the Netherlands, the DEI must protect itself. An action is put into place whereby German nationals in the DEI who are thought to be sympathizers of the Nazi regime are rounded up and placed in internment camps, so that the Nazi actions can be monitored. As Jaap works for a German company, there are effects that are felt with his work.

With concerns about the European situation, daily activities in Medan continue. Work continues, and families continue to grow. A sign of Jaap's growing prosperity is the acquisition of his driver's license, so that he can obtain his own car. Jaap receives his driver's license in Medan, Sumatra on August 15, 1940. It is issued for a five-year period, expiring August 15, 1945.

MODEL XVI (WEGVERKEERSBESLUIT-V. EN W.).

Afgegeven aan J. Bebelaar

geboren te Rotterdam

den 9 den Mei 1911

van beroep Boekhouder n.v. Carl Schlieper

wonende ~~tijdelijk verblijf houdende~~ te Medan

Heemskerklaan no 18

Dit rijbewijs is uitgereikt te Medan

op den 15 den Aug 1940 en is

mitsdien geldig tot den 15/8 1945

De ~~Gouverneur~~ / Resident van der Oostkust van Sumatra

Voor dezen

De Hoofdcommissaris van Politie,

op last

De Commissaris van Politie 1e Kl

Voor dezen:

De

1939 — 1½ G. — ZEGEL VAN NED INDIE

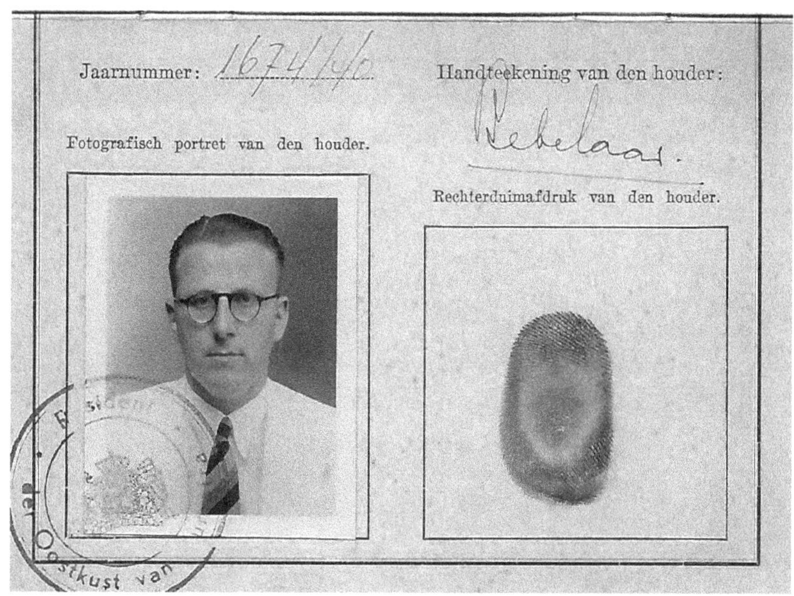

With the Germans occupying the Netherlands, communication with the family is hard. Jaap and Bé take to writing a letter to a pastor friend in France, who in turn sends a letter to Bé's parents to give them information about the family.

Morges, Grand Rue 98 bis

Dear Mr and Mrs

Finally, I can give you some news of your son and his family. I received a letter today in which is written that all three are doing well and that they are happy with news from you. The little boy, Wouter Jan, is cute and never cries. He is very healthy, born on April 28 at 9.30 minus 3 minutes and weighing 3 kg, 550 grams. Now, at 6 months – the letter is dated 12 November – he weighs more than 8 kg. He has blue eyes and blond hair. They say he looks like his father. Andre already gave him, for more than 4 months, rice once a day; after 2 weeks, two times and now he also eats coulis. He has been vaccinated in October, he can sit down and has 2 teeth. Your children think of you a lot and hope to get a letter from you with news. You can write to me and I will give them your news.

We are okay, we ourselves, and we are starting to live our new life in Morges. I make a lot of music, singing and violin; that fills the time very well. All our children are very well. Hoping that you and yours are healthy. I send you, dear Mr and Mrs, our very best wishes,

Otto B.

Pastor.

4 December 1940.

1941

The war in Europe continues. Tensions in the Pacific are starting to mount. The Dutch East Indies still has many internees who are of German descent, since the invasion of the Netherlands in May 1940. As a member of the Dutch army, since 1931, Jaap's records are transferred to the DEI. In April 1941, he finds it necessary to resign from his position with his employer. Since hostilities have started in Europe, his company has been sold to Java Steel.

Medan, 28 April 1941

To: Mr. Jac Bebelaar Esq.

Medan, Sumatra

From: Personnel of Java Steel, Medan

Dear Mr. Bebelaar Esq:

We remember very well the first day you arrived here and our hope that you would stay with us for many years. Alas, after 2 years you have to leave us. In those 2 years we found you to a be diligent, honest, accurate person. In your words, sometime strict, but nevertheless with a warm heart and always willing to support your staff, in the office as well as in private. We have learned a great deal from you, especially in the department of bookkeeping. May 10, 1940 was a very dark day, but we continued to work together. We shall not forget.

There is a time of coming and a time of leaving. Be assured that we will not forget you. Please accept this small token of our thanks, a silver cigarette case. A present from your personnel. See attached list of names. In addition, from the bookkeeping department, this photograph of the staff. We hope you will often use the cigarette case and find a place at your home for the photograph.

We wish you all the best in your career, and best wishes for you and your family.

Medan, 28 April 1941

Personnel of Java Steel Medan

Attachment: List of names

List of people who contributed to the silver cigarette case:

1. Mevr. Goud
2. Juffr. Parker
3. Holwerda
4. Tan Tjoei The
5. Tan Tjoei Tin
6. Tjong Fie Tjoan
7. Anwar
8. R. Machmoed
9. Ghouse
10. Hoesin (Belawan)
11. Gho Tiauw Hong
12. Tjioe Tek Soei
13. Jap Fook Chong
14. Hoesin (Boe)
15. Atan
16. Talib
17. Oemar (Loo~er)
18. Oemar (Boe)
19. Djafar Sidik
20. Adenan
21. Toegiman
22. Sjarief (Teha)
23. Abas
24. Boestamam
25. Djohar
26. Bahroen
27. Barned
28. Maradja
29. Moedji
30. Satimin
31. Gomar
32. Haroen
33. Bais
34. Massot
35. Bakri
36. Idris
37. Lucas
38. Noer
39. Asrah
40. Saiman

41. Limin
42. Aboe Bakar
43. Moh. Sjarief

Jaap and Wouter in the yard in Medan 1941

Proud moments for a father, walking with his son.

Family Portrait 1941

N.V. Javasche Ijzer-En Staalhandel October 14, 1941

Undersigned hereby declare that Lord Jac. Bebelaar of 14 May 1936 to end of April 1941 as accountant has been employed by the N.V. Carl Schlieper Trade Me (later N.V. Java Iron and Steel Trade) and belong engaged in work assigned to him.

His last salary was f. 375 per month.

Mr. Bebelaar was granted at his own request, dismissal.

Signed, October 14, 1941, Batavia

E.G. Drenth W.L.H. Hubregtse

Jaap is now back in the military, as the Dutch have German internees to watch over.

December 7, 1941

This fateful day, the Japanese bombs Pearl Harbour in Hawaii, as well as Singapore Harbour. This act of aggression launches World War II in the Pacific region. The Dutch East Indies army is now becoming fully mobilized, ready to defend the territory they call home, from any attacks by the Japanese.

1942

The world is now at war. In Europe, Germany is the country all are fighting. In the Pacific, Japan is the aggressor. Germany and Japan have formed an alliance to dominate their own specific regions of the world. With this in mind, in January 1942, the Dutch East Indies government determines it is best to remove the Germans they have interned and send them to India to be placed in the hands of the

British. To carry out this action four merchant marine ships are loaded with German prisoners, KNIL (Royal Netherlands Indies) soldiers and the merchant mariners. The first three ships successfully make it to India. The last ship, the Van Imhoff, is torpedoed by a Japanese fighter jet early into its journey. The *Van Imhoff* sinks 110 miles off the west coast of Sumatra.

There is very little family communication from this time period. The whereabouts of Jaap is not known, and the situation with Bé and Wouter is also not known.

Bé finally receives communication regarding Jaap. It is comforting and disturbing at the same time. It also provides information as to the location of Bé and Wouter.

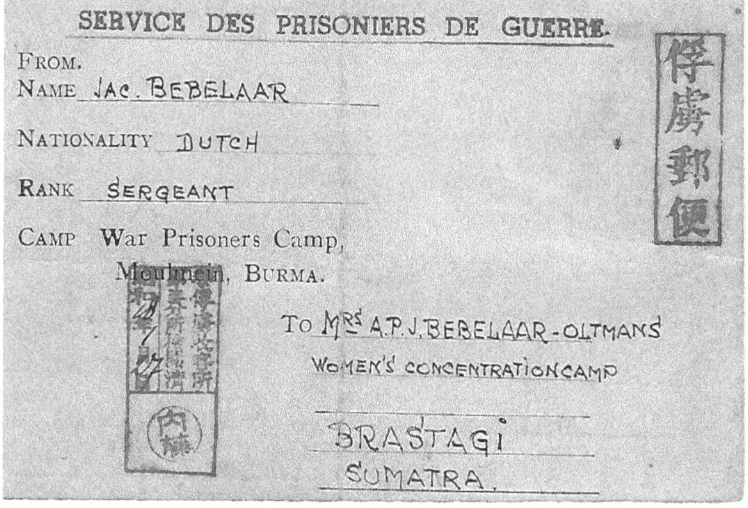

SERVICE DES PRISONIERS DE GUERRE.

俘虜郵便

FROM.
NAME JAC. BEBELAAR
NATIONALITY DUTCH
RANK SERGEANT
CAMP War Prisoners Camp,
Moulmein, BURMA.

To Mrs A.P.J. BEBELAAR-OLTMANS
WOMEN'S CONCENTRATIONCAMP
BRASTAGI
SUMATRA.

IMPERIAL JAPANESE ARMY.

I am interned at The War Prisoners Camp at Moulmein in Burma.

My health is (good, ~~usual, poor~~)

I have not had any illness.

~~I (am) (have been) in~~ hospital.

I am ~~(not)~~ working (for pay at 15 CENTS per day).

~~My salary is per month.~~

I am with friends COR BRUGMAN AND Mr WEISFELT, W.J. DRIESSEN.

ALWAYS I'M THINKING OF YOU AND OUR LITTLE WOUTER JAN.

HOPE TO GET SOON ANY NEWS FROM YOU. MANY KISSES.

From Jaap Bebelaar.

Bé now knows that Jaap is in Burma. The timeframe when this is received is unknown. Other than Bé, the family is not aware of where Jaap is.

Bé receives a second communication from Jaap. It appears that it could be four months later. It is a controlled message by the Japanese with little real communication allowed for the loved ones.

SERVICE DES PRISONERS DE GUERRE.

FROM P. O. W. No. 59[illegible]

NAME BEBELAAR, J.

NATIONALITY DUTCH

RANK SERGEANT

Camp: War Prisoners Camp,
Moulmein, BURMA.

To Mrs A.P.J. BEBELAAR-OLTMANS
WOMEN-CONCENTRATION CAMP
P.S.Y.
BRASTAGI
SUMATRA'S EAST-COAST

IMPERIAL JAPANESE ARMY.

I am still in a P. O. W. Camp near Moulmein, Burma, There are 20,000 Prisoners, being Australian, Dutch, English, and American. There are several camps of 2/3000 prisoners who work at settled labour daily.

We are quartered in very plain huts. The climate is good. Our life is now easier with regard to food, medicine and clothes. The Japanese Commander sincerely endeavours to treat prisoners kindly.

Officers' salary is based on salary of Japanese Officers of the same rank and every prisoner who performs labour or duty is given daily wages from 25 cents (minimum) to 45 cents, according to rank and work.

Canteens are established where we can buy some extra foods and smokes. By courtesy of the Japanese Commander we conduct concerts in the camps, and a limited number go to a picture show about once per month.

HOPE YOU AND WOUTERJAN STILL O.K. WITH ME ALSO GOOD. EXPECT RATHER SOON WE WILL BE TOGETHER. Jaap.

1943

1943 goes without communication until the family in the Netherlands receives the following message from the Red Cross:

NETHERLANDS RED CROSS

The Hague Nov. 18, 1943

Mr. J. J. Oltmans

Heidelaan 3 Bennekom

Hereby I inform you that a message was received from our Tokyo information office that J. Bebelaar, Sgt. Infantry is present in the prison camp in Thailand. This telegram was sent from Tokyo on Oct. 6, 1943.

Head Information Bureau Netherlands Red Cross.

1944

In 1944, Jaap's father sends the following letter be Bé's father:

To: Mr. and Mrs. Oltmans-Bemond   Rotterdam, 29 August 1944

Heidelaan 3

Bennekom

Dear family:

Thank you so much for your letter yesterday, because we received no news about Jaap. And now we are worrying about Bé and the little one. The situation with us is the same. And we can do nothing for her. We could not think this last week, Thursday, when we were so pleasantly together.

Tomorrow I will go to the office of the Red Cross (to confirm Jaap's death) and at the same time I will have the cards printed to send to everyone who should know. Can you send us the list of your acquaintances and addresses and we will send cards to them. A draft of the announcement goes with this letter, and we think you will agree with the text.

Our heartfelt condolences with this sad loss. With cordial greeting.

Yours

D. Bebelaar and L.W. Bebelaar v.d. Voort

Draft Announcement:

We received the terrible news that on 22 June 1943 in Thailand-camp passed away our dear son and son-in-law, Jacob Bebelaar, at the age of 32 years.

We hope that his wife and son are strong to courageously accept this loss.

On behalf of all brothers and sisters:

Rotterdam   D. Bebelaar

Beukelsweg 94 L.W. Bebelaar v.d. Voort

Bennekom J.J. Oltmans

Heidelaan 3~ A. Oltmans - Bemond

Ons bereikte de ontstellende mededeeling, dat op 22 Juni 1943 in Thaicamp is overleden onze geliefde zoon en schoonzoon

Jacob Bebelaar

in den leeftijd van 32 jaar.

Wij hopen, dat zijn vrouw en zoon gesterkt mogen worden dit verlies moedig te dragen, hetgeen ons een troost zal zijn.

Augustus 1944.

Mede namens broers en zusters :

ROTTERDAM, Beukelsweg 94. — D. BEBELAAR. L. W. BEBELAAR-v. d. Voort.

BENNEKOM, Heidelaan 3. — J. J. OLTMANS. A. OLTMANS-Bémond.

1945

1945 is a year that will change the world forever.

In Europe, the hostilities come to an end on May 10, 1945. However, the Pacific war continues. The United States takes action to end the war with the dropping of two atomic bombs over Japan. As a result, the Japanese forces surrender on August 15, 1945.

This is also the day that Jaap's driver's license in Sumatra expires. The family in the Netherlands is now desperately seeking information about the whereabouts and condition of Bé and Wouter.

Below are the requests for information David Bebelaar sent to the Red Cross in Rotterdam.

Application for information

Person sought: Bebelaar Oltmans

First Name: Andrea Pieternella Johanna

Date of Birth: 11 Oct. 1911

Widow of Jacob Bebelaar
Children: Wouter Jan Bebelaar

Date of birth: 28 April 1940 at Medan

Last known address: Sumatra prison camp
Before: Heemskerklaan 18, Medan

Requested by: Bebelaar, David, Beukelsweg 94 Rotterdam

Father-in-Law:

Person sought: Wouter Jan Bebelaar

Date of Birth: 28 April 1940

Son of Jacob Bebelaar and A.P.J. Bebelaar-Oltmans
Last known address: Sumatra prison camp

Requested by: Bebelaar, David of Beukelsweg 94 Rotterdam

Grandfather

Bé's parents receive a letter from her and are relieved and happy.

Bennekom Oct 30th, 1945

Dear Andre and Woutertje,

We were so happy with your letter of last Sep 16th in which we could see that you and Woutertje are OK, but that you still have not heard anything from Jaap.

We have tried several times to get news about you with the help of the Red Cross, but every time with no result until we finally heard that you and Woutertje are now in a concentration camp in Sumatra and that Jaap was in Camp Thai in Thailand, as a prisoner of war. Later on, we got this news once again and we could send letters to him. We wrote him a long letter right away, of course, and asked him to write you that we are OK here. We never heard back from him, however, and we had to do with what we read in the newspapers, and there was not much good written about Thailand. There were a great number of prisoners sick and many died.

It is now almost 8 years ago that you left for Indie and so much happened in all those years. On Nov 7th the first plane will leave for Indie with mail from here and this is a short note to let you know how we are doing. This plane will take 5 days to get there and so you will receive this letter around Nov 15th. What we have experienced here is pretty bad.

Mama and I are healthy. We were right in this war and we had to evacuate to Ede and we ended up in a colony for mentally challenged children where it was not too bad compared with other people who had to live in garages and chicken runs.

Kor and Herre and the kids are all OK. Bram has been appointed Notary in Goedereede and their family has a new member: Jan Jacob, a very darling boy.

In Rotterdam all is also OK and in the mean time they have 2 more boys. We regularly keep in contact with them and we speak with them sometimes. This is a short account of us. Mama also likes to write to you and so I will end this letter.

Bye dear Bé and Wouterje. Try to keep well and I hope to hear from you soon.

Bye for now and I wish you the best and a big hug and kiss for you and Wouterje.

Your Dad.

Bennekom, 30 October 1945

Dear Bé,

When we came home from Kor and Herre's – where we stayed for one week – we found your letter. We were so happy to see your handwriting and read that you and the little Wouter are OK. We were very worried and could read from your writing that you have not received our letter we sent to you through the Red Cross. We would love to see a picture of our grandson. I am sure you had a very difficult time, and it is so awful that we could not help you.

We also had a very bad time. Starting Sep 17 when the allied troops arrived in the Betuwe it all started and Bennekom was often a target. That meant either find shelter or lie flat on the floor. We also had someone here, a lady from The Hague, who had to leave her house and also some refugees. These people were named van Raalten, their son and family are in a camp in Sumatra. Then we received the order that we all had to leave Bennekom within 12 hours. We had no transportation and we could only take the bare necessities with us and with help of friends a little more. We spent 7 months in a colony-home half an hour from Ede. We were there with 4 families in a big hall, but all went well. Dad was ill there and was 4 weeks in hospital North with a stomach problem. When Bennekom was safe again we found our home looted. It was not to describe chaos, but we managed and got through this. We lost a lot of weight, but we are getting better. All is well with Kor and Herre. They also went through a fearful period with all those bombardments. Luckily, they are alive. There is a chance that we will temporarily go to America. Bram and Nel are also OK. Their youngest is a very nice boy. Kor and Harre's kids are also very nice, especially Janneke. Nel has a very nice house in a nice area. She just visited us and she looks very healthy. The islands have had no shortage of food, only *once in a while a bomb blast. And yet, they had hard times when Jantje was born. Bram had to go to Goeree and Nel was so tired and the connection was so bad. But all is well now.*

We will have to tell so much when we see each other again. Aunt Annet and Uncle have had a lot of sorrow. The twins were sent to Germany; they had helped Jews. Neeltje came home very ill and Eloise died. Luckily, they received good news of Egbert. Nel Pfeiffer has sent good news. Piet de Groen died in action in Russia; he enlisted in the German army and the entire family was shocked.

Now you know the most important things here, Bé. We are now longing for a letter from you. We constantly think of you. I hope that you can receive our good news. Bye darling. A big kiss for you and for my little Woutertje.

The following day, Bé's parents struggle with the news they know about Jaap, but understand from Bé's letter, that she does not know the circumstances. They write again.

Bennekom, Nov. 1 '45

Dearest Bé,

After we wrote you and thought it over seriously, we thought it better to tell you the truth, although it might be hard for you to accept. You wrote that you were hoping to see Jaap again. But dearest we got news way back in August 1944 from the Red Cross that Jaap died in Camp Thai on June 22, 1943 due to dysentery. We know, Bé, that this is a big blow for you and are very sorry that we cannot help and comfort you. Try to be courageous and think about your little boy who needs you even more now. We kept on hoping that they might have made a mistake, as it has happened before. At the Lijten's they received a death notice for Neeltje while she was recuperating at home and Ab Carrier did receive news of the passing of his wife, while that is not true. He married for the second time. Can you imagine what kind of confusion that brings? But as since long we did not receive any news to the contrary we have to believe that it is true. I do hope that you do receive our long letter at the same time as this one. I did send, as well, a letter along with first lieutenant D van Raalten who left a month ago for Indonesia.

Stay strong Bé. Our thoughts are always with you and we hope you will be with us very soon.

With our best regards and

a big kiss for you and your little darling

Dad and Mom

Bé is now receiving a steady stream of correspondence from the family. Her sister Nel writes:

Goedereede, 6 Nov. 1945

Darling Bé

We were so happy to receive your letter and that Woutertje is in good health, too. That must have been a horrible time in that camp. Is there a possibility that you can soon come back to the Netherlands? For father and mother, it was also a joy to receive your letter, especially after the hard times they had. We were shocked to learn from your letter that you did not know yet that Jaap had died. By now you must have heard from the Red Cross. Dear Bé, what a sorrow for you. And Jaap was still so young. You will be so happy that you have Woutertje and look after him. Is he a darling little boy? Who does he look like? When you are up to it, we hope you will write us a long letter about everything, and we long to have you back home.

Father and mother have had a hard time. Their house was looted empty and vandalized. They were evacuated for a while, etc. They have aged so much. Father is slowly getting better, but mother is still very thin. She is often sad. Bram is now Notary in Goedereede. In January we will have been here two years. We live in a large Notary house with a beautiful garden. We were lucky that we moved away from Zeeland Flanders because the battles there were the worst in Europe. The village of Groede was the center of the Red Cross aid, but nevertheless parts of Groede were bombed. The villages around Groede were all destroyed: Oostburg, Sluis, etc. But we will tell you about it at a later time.

We now have three children. Gon, you have seen. She is now 10 years old and very independent. All by herself she travels to family or friends to stay there for a few days, etc. She wears her hair in two braids and she is a lovely, active, girl. Then there is Tek. He is now 8 years old. Loves his mom, but he is a rascal, a lovely rascal. Then the pride of the family, Jan Jacob. He was born on New Year's Eve, and in December he will be 2 years old. Thus, born in the war years. He is a darling. A blond, skinny kid with a darling little face, bright, smart because he is teased often by the older siblings. He is a real war child. He eats anything. Especially in the hunger winter he ate anything. There was no milk, no sugar. Gon and Tek also survived it. When the men 40 years old or younger were taken away, Bram was just 41 and could stay home. Often, I was very worried. There were some scary times, but we survived.

Three weeks ago, I visited Kor. Heere was in America. I had not seen Kor in two and a half years and Janneke and Tjeerd, not in four years. It was so good to be together again. I could get a ride in an automobile because taking the train is very difficult. You have to go in freight cars. All bridges have been destroyed. But one good thing is you don't have to be afraid of bombardments. We live close to Rotterdam and we can go up and down in one day for the shopping. Some of the shops are still quite empty. There is no piece of clothing in the clothing shops. Fortunately, there is light, electricity. We had to have candles in the evening. The winter evenings were quite long, and you were home all the time because of the curfew. There is no money yet. We live with coupons. Dear younger sister of mine. I am going to end this letter. Be strong. We think of you all the time and we long for you to be here. Bye for now Bébel. Many greetings from Bram, Gon, Tek and Jan and kisses from your sister NEL.

Bé is getting all the news from the Netherlands, about how everyone managed through the war. For the first time, she receives correspondence regarding Jaap, from a fellow POW in Burma, a gentleman who came to the Dutch East Indies aboard the same ship as Jaap did in 1936: Henk Moddemeyer, Sgt. 157912.

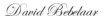

Singapore November 24, 1945, Camp Princess Irene

Dear Bé,

Yesterday I received your letter. It was a pleasant surprise for me. As a matter of fact, I had inquired after you and yesterday, received at the same time as I received your letter, a form with your address. Until then I did not know if you were still alive and if you knew about Jaap's death. Your letter was in fact an answer to many questions. I am glad to hear that you and Woutertje are doing well. You did not have it too easy, although you are were lucky to be in a cool climate for a while. For me, it was a big blow when I heard that Jaap had passed. He was always one of my best friends. We were together in Burma for a long time.

We were shipped on May 15, 1942 from Belawan and ended up, after several stops, in Tavoy in Burma.

After that we worked together on the railway dike. Jaap was seldom sick, he only had a light case of beri. Later on, we stayed under real bad conditions in camp km. 108 on the rail line. Here he got dysentery and he kept on working for too long. At that time, I was not there anymore because I did get typhus and was send off to the base hospital. Jaap never did refuse to work. When the doctor asked he would still try to work. That is why he was already really exhausted when he contracted dysentery. Therefore, he did not make it through.

A friend of ours, Ras (military sergeant), had been with him from the beginning of the war and was with him when he passed on. He still has a few things from Jaap, which he wants to give you.

He does not want to write you as he is not sure where you are and if you know that Jaap passed away.

Send him a letter. His address is now military sergeant Th. Ras, Sabang, N. Sumatra

You better do that yourself, then you will receive a message sooner from him, and I can imagine that you find this important.

Jaap stayed the same until the end and he always did think about others. He was not selfish, which just about everybody was. In the evenings, we did mention you and Woutertje quite often. I have visited his gravesite several times later on. He is resting quietly under the trees of the jungle and has a nice cross with an engraved inscription on his gravesite. I understand how you do feel when you read this. Cry out loud and be proud of Jaap. You can be proud of him. May this be of some comfort to you and lessen the emptiness that has come around you. But there is one thing that I am sure of that Jaap would not like – that you keep being sad. Keep your head up and try to still make the best of your life. Heavens that is not too bad. Get out of this chaotic situation. I think it is right that you want to go to Holland. A change of environment will do you good. Holland is not everything either, but it will still be easier to get through it than here.

We always got along very well and confidentially with each other. See me as your brother. When I knew that Jaap had passed on, I did take it upon myself as my task to help you with anything. Do not feel ashamed. If I can do anything for you, how absurd it may seem to look like, tell me. I will gladly do it. You may lean on me! I do really feel a "darned" sorrow for you. If you know that you will stop here on your travels, I hope to hear from you. You will not be coming in a tented camp here but in houses in camp Wilhelmina or in big buildings in Camp Princess Irene. It is pretty good here. We have got money and can buy ourselves what we need. After Burma, I was in Thailand and then 1 ½ years in Indo China. We were liberated in Saigon and I was quite happy there. On October the 16th we arrived in Singapore, where I did get a light bacterial dysentery and ended up in the hospital. I am completely cured now and am staying in Camp Irene, and from here I go every now and then to Singapore to have a good time. I do hope to get paid for my services and to go on leave to Holland. For the time being, I am not doing any work. I do want to get out there. I still feel quite restless. I still feel enclosed. Fortunately, I am slowly getting over it with amusement. To party it out is the best remedy. I do hope to get married someday because the bachelor's situation does not please me anymore. I did get to know a nice girl here (as well, 32 yrs old), who just arrived from Mexico. She is the sister of a friend of mine. She does not know it yet, but maybe it will work out. I would be pleased.

Okay, Bé, write me sometime. Be open minded and try to find distraction. Come over soon, then we can talk and go out. Kind regards as well to Woutertje and wishing you strength.

Yours, Henk

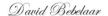

For the first time, Bé now has information about when Jaap went to Burma, where he was located, his state of health and the cause of his death. She can be proud of the fact that Jaap was someone who never refused work and took on extra duties to help others.

Bé sets out to contact Sgt. Ras, who had been with Jaap from the beginning of the military service in 1942.

More news comes to Bé from her parents, about Jaap's brother Dick.

Bennekom, 28 Nov. 1945

Darling Bé,

We waited anxiously for a letter from you, but the airplane that arrived last Saturday only had a little bit of mail. We anxiously wait for more news from you. How are you and how is Woutertje? Are you both in good health? Could you write a long letter about you and your little boy? Here, things are good. Father and I gained a little bit of weight. We were a skinny pair, but we survived. I wish you were here and that we could help you with your sorrow and together find a new beginning. I heard from Gerda. She often writes us and sometimes visits us. She is not at her old job anymore but takes care of the household of a widowed or divorced man (I don't know) with a little son. She wrote that they will marry on December 14. Riet van Dongen is getting married on December 4. They will rent a couple of furnished rooms in Amsterdam. The furniture stores are still empty, thus young couples rent furnished. Her spouse-to-be is a chemist at a beer brewery. Nel and Bram, now that they live in Goeree, often visit the van Dongen family. We heard from the Bebelaar family the sad news that Dick died in the camp in Thailand. The Bebelaar family heard the news from Henk van Tol, who was also in that camp. So much sad news. And how would to be. So far, the winter has been quite mild. We only have a little bit of coal for heating.

We all sit in the smallest room with a small stove that is also used for cooking. We also have a bit of wood that father is now cutting up. You will be so cold when you are back here, especially the little Wouter who has always been in a warm land. The food supply is now much. There are things like matches, cleaning supplies, and the like, with shortages, but there is enough bread and we manage with other things, for example 400 grams of sugar per week, 3 ounces of meat (Note: I ounce is 100 grams). We make do. Occasionally the heavily hit areas receive something extra. For example, next Tuesday they will receive a pound of jam (Note: a pound is 500 grams, half a kilo). Most things are very expensive and can only be purchased with special coupons. Father badly needed shoes and fortunately could get a pair from someone else. So, slowly things get better. Darling Bé, we hope to hear from you soon. We think of you so much and long to have you here. Dear child. Be strong. Many greetings for both of you and many kisses.

Your father and mother.

PS I, with Nel, Bram, Kor, Herre and children, all is well. Herre is back from America and brought many things for his family. For us, he ordered three packages with oodstuffs ordered in America. We wait to see what it is. Bye.

PS 2 Did you receive our previous letters, Bé? Kiss from father. And a big kiss for Woutertje. Bye.

Bennekom, 9 December 1945

Darling Bé,

We are looking forward to your next letter. We are so happy that you and Woutertje are in good health. You didn't say where you are at the moment. We think in Medan. You wrote you are trying to straighten things out there. Mrs. Baruch was interned in a camp in Brastagi. She is now back in Holland and spoke on the radio. Were you in the same camp?

Here, the food supply is getting better. Compared with a year ago, it is royal. I shudder when I think back to the food at that time. Everyday a bit of potato and cold vegetable, no meat. Government supplied bread and rye, ground with water. Now we also receive something extra from the Red Cross in America, Denmark, Africa, Ireland, etc., only for the hard-hit areas. That is us. This week we received a pound (half a kilo) butter and a tin of jam.

It is very cold, and we only heat the small front room with so little coal or firewood we have. We got some furniture to put in there. Jaap Oltmans from Utrecht, he is still a bachelor, sent us a double bed with mattress and pillows and a 2-person wash table, a few cups, a few knives. And for father, a suit and some underwear. In the beginning, I was very down that our house was plundered, but worse things have happened to others.

Did I write that Eltien Krijtle died in a concentration camp? One can say she was tortured to death.

Nel Pfeiffer is in Batavia and helps out at the palace of the Governor General. And Egbert and his German wife are also well. Much has happened in the 8 years that you have been away. We are a pair of old people. The war years have left their mark. But we feel fit and healthy.

Woutertje looks a fine young boy. On the photograph he is only a year and a half. Nel's youngest, Jan Jacob, is skinnier, and also blond like Wouter. Iek is a sturdy boy, just like Bram. You won't recognize your nephews and nieces. And the Bebelaar family has two more boys. Cousin Wouter is older than the uncle. Fine children. David, now called Dave, likes to camp in this area and always visits us then. He is a nice boy, pleasant. With Christmas, we plan to go to Goeree. I am not looking forward to the trip. Traveling is still difficult. Trains are over full, and busses have long waiting lines. But it is improving. In our neighbourhood here, we celebrated St. Nicholas. Father was St. Nicholas. All dressed up and make-up. We often thought of Woutertje. He will enjoy these parties for children when he is back in the Netherlands. I am writing this letter on a Sunday morning, with a cup of real coffee. I just spilled a drop on this letter. Excuse the spot. Yesterday, with a coupon, we got half an ounce (50 gram) of real tea for this afternoon. How is this in the Indies? Enough tea and coffee? Darling Bé, I end this letter, looking forward to your letters. Bye Bé, many greetings and kisses. From mother.

PS Bye, Woutertje. Will you come soon to opa and oma in Holland? Kisses from opa and oma. We long for you to be here.

Bennekom, Dec. 10 '45

Darling Bé,

We were so happy with your letter of 15 Nov., arriving Dec. 2. The cards you received from us were sent many months ago. We thought you would never receive it. We already knew that Jaap died. The chairman of the Red Cross told us personally. He is a friend of ours. We cannot comprehend that we won't see our dear Jaap again. And why. We wrote you two letters. In the first one we did not say that we knew. You know mistakes are made. Mama wrote you a second letter that we knew. Now you have received both letters. We had been told earlier that Jaap was in Thailand and that we could write him. But it was already a year ago that he died.

We can imagine how great a loss this is for you and the little Wouter. We know so little about Wouter. On the photo he is a darling. Only 1 ½ years old. He looks like Tjeerd, when Tjeerd was that age.

There are so many people who are in a similar situation. Be courageous, Bé. That is also best for Wouter. If you want to come here (you will be most welcome), we can help you. There are several ships now that repatriate the Dutch back to Holland. Widows and orphans get priority. Everything will be taken care off. In Cairo, you will receive winter clothing. When arriving in Holland, nobody is allowed to meet you. You will be driven to our house by car. We have a large house and you can stay here. In a beautiful part of Holland. We will be good for Wouter and will try to give him what Jaap would have been for him. The Dutch government and many volunteer associations will assist financially and materially. For now, each Dutch national from Indie receives 150 florin per month and a child under 7 years old receives 60 florin per month, and when older than 7 years receives 100 florin per month.

Where are you at the moment? Are you still in the camp? On the letter you only wrote Medan, no other address information. And do you get enough to eat? Here in Holland, it is good. We receive coupons to buy the necessities. Great help from America, Sweden, Norway, Switzerland, etc.

I can keep writing forever Bé, but I will stop now. Be strong, Bé. Love. Kisses, also for Wouter. Father.

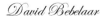

A letter from Bé's eldest sister, Kor:

Eindhoven, 11 Dec. 1945

Darling Bé and darling Woutertje,

When we heard about a year and a half ago that Jaap had died and heard that he died a year earlier we were totally shocked and upset. We always loved Jaap very much. He was still so young. We couldn't believe it. And for you, it must be terrible and dreadful. We can imagine it because here in Holland terrible things have also happened. Many died in concentration camps or were executed.

Bé, we wish you strength. We always thought of you and Woutertje. And Jaap, we remember as a fine and warm man. We hope that Woutertje has that same sunny and friendly character from his father. On the photo, he is a darling little boy. He looks a bit like Tjeerd with that white blond hair and a mouth full of teeth. Tjeerd used to be a bit heavy, but now he is very skinny. And never sick, except for the children sicknesses. He has something tender in him. I had that too. Janneke is sturdier and a handy person. Janneke is now 10 years old and Tjeerd is almost 9. Janneke has blond curls. She is now in the fourth grade at school. Tjeerd is in third grade.

The children survived the war years, physically and mentally. Physical was difficult. We had little food, and we had to purchase it at exorbitant prices. Mentally they were strong. You hear of children who are hurt mentally, from bombardments for example.

Father and mother have lost everything, but you know that already. They manage. Father, especially, is strong. Mother has aged a lot. But if everything returns to normal, so will they. They long for your return to Holland and, of course, for Wouter. Much has been destroyed or damaged in the Netherlands, but everybody is full of courage to rebuild. In the newspaper you read that foreigners, American and English, who visit Amsterdam comment on this courage.

And you have to tell us how you suffered in the Japanese concentration camps. We hear horrible things. But, is it all true?

In a bombardment, the house of aunt Lien and uncle Kees was hit. Fortunately, they survived. They now live with Rein and Lineke.

Rein and Lineke are expecting a baby. Adri and Jos are in a concentration camp for NSB people (Note: NSB is the Dutch Nazi party, collaborators with the Germans). The children are with Jos's parents. Koen and Aaltje also lost everything. They, too, have a baby. The Krythe's have survived and are well to do. For most, the situation is sad. ETtien has died in Germany. Neeltje came back from Germany but is very ill. I don't know, did Father and Mother write this already to you? Herre's family came through it all right. Herre's mother is well, 82 years old.

When you are back in the Netherlands and I can help you, don't hesitate to ask. Dear Bé, be strong. We wait for you with open arms. We will do everything for you and Woutertje. Kisses for Woutertje from his aunt and greetings and kisses for you from all of us.

Your Kor.

Bé finally hears from Sgt. Ras.

Singapore, Dec 24, 1945

Dear Mrs. Bebelaar,

Very regrettably during the short time that I was in Medan, I could not visit you to tell you personally some things about Jaap.

As you might remember, we already became friends in Kabanjahe, north of Medan and we did stay together from then on. Jaap was a very good friend of mine, and he was always a great help for everybody. Even when we were sick and had to walk from camp 70 on the Burma rail track to camp 108, he did help out the others with carrying. Up until camp 70 he was always fit. However, in camp 108, in early June, he caught a very serious bout of malaria. When he was just about over it, he did get dysentery. His body had been weakened severely by the malaria, and it could not take anymore.

On June 22, 1943 at 4.45 in the afternoon he passed on. I was there. At 3 o'clock he was still conscious when I was at his side. Although he was in good spirits, he likely felt that he would not make it.

He asked me specifically to tell you that he was passing on in "rest and peace" with himself. And that is indeed what happened. He became unconscious shortly after and passed on calm and peacefully, without regaining consciousness. For myself, it was a big blow to lose a good friend under these horrible circumstances at that time, and I can imagine how much he meant to you both.

I am sorry that because of circumstances, our original plan to come and visit you in Medan is not possible. By us, I mean Messrs. Paulus van Frese, Hoogeweg, Groeneveld, Buijs and myself.

As well, my unexpected, sudden departure from Medan made a personal relay to you of what happened not possible, however I do hope to tell you more, some time in the future, personally.

Furthermore, I still have in my possession some personal objects from Jaap, like a lighter, 5 pictures and a frame. His ring, which I did have, has been stolen from me during a sudden inspection by the Japanese on August 29, 1943. I had his ring with a drawing from him and some keys hidden in a center lamp. But on that day, all center lamps were taken away, and as much as I tried to get them back, we were powerless and we did not succeed. I am sorry that it happened, especially for you, and that I cannot hand you over these personal items.

I did talk to Moddemeyer here, who, like yourself, is going to Holland, and it might be better that I give the lighter and pictures for him to take along. If you agree to it, then I will hand it over personally. Possibly, I could also give it to somebody going to Medan, however this is not that easy, as fewer travel from here to Medan.

On Jaap's gravesite is a simple wooden sign with the inscription Military sergeant 1st class J. Bebelaar, June 22, 1943. The physician who treated Jaap is Dr. In 't Veld. At the gravesite, Mayor De Vries (being the Camp commander) spoke, Captain Smit, as acting minister, was the second speaker.

While Lieutenant Paulus was the third person, he spoke on behalf of Frese, Hoogeweg. We made wreaths from flowers and plants out of the jungle and there were three beautiful wreaths, one from you, one from his friends and one from the camp commander, Mayor de Vries. The coffin was covered with the Dutch flag and after the speeches the National Anthem "het Wilhelmus" was sung, after which all present made the military salute.

I do hope that I have given you an impression with this short relay of what happened and that although circumstances were very bad, everything possible was done to have the funeral as solemnly as possible.

Furthermore, I would like to wish you the strength in the year ahead and a good stay in Holland with Woutertje. Jaap told me often about him, and I hope that you will have the strength to carry this loss.

With kind regards and hoping to meet you some day in the future.

Pleased to be of your service, (Signed) Dorus Ras

Camp Irene, 27-12-45

Dear Bé,

If you receive this letter still in time I hope to wish you all the best for the new year, and maybe there might be, somewhere in this world, a bit of good luck for you. As for me, no more, because I did get it already, Bé.

As a matter of fact, I did get engaged to Willy Hoopman on Christmas Day. She is 19 years of age and very sweet. We love each other very much and are looking ahead to a rosy future. We are going both to Holland as soon as possible and are going to get married there. We will see you there. Ras is here. I did talk to him, and he is going to take Jaap's personal items to Holland. He will write to you in Holland.

I am very busy, and I do hope that you do not mind that I end this letter now. Bé, stay strong and I wish you all the best for the rest of your life and as well for Woutertje, yours

Henk

P.S. If I can do anything for you, please let me know. Bye.

Singapore, December 28th, 1945

Dear Mrs. Bebelaar,

I did receive your second letter after a long delay. It was addressed to Sabang, while I am in Singapore now, That is why it was delayed.

Furthermore, you have given me a military rank which I don't have, so that was hard for the mail service here. Also, my initials are DMJ. I hope that your next letter will get here faster. The "S. S. Noordam" doesn't go through Singapore? I would like to talk to you before your departure to the Netherlands. But it is so hard to express yourself clearly on paper. I hope that I did as you would have wished. I gave Jaap's sunglasses and glasses to the medical doctor, who gave them to people who needed them badly. There were many people who lost their glasses and needed them urgently. I don't think I mentioned it in my last letter, but I will mail it to you as you would like. There is a diary, in which I made notations in Burma, a brief description of the funeral and things that Jaap left behind and who has them or had them.

How are you doing, yourself? I am with little Woutertje. I wish you the best for the coming year.

With kind regards, as well from my wife, who I believe you don't know?

Dorus Ras

Sumatra Planters' Unit Singapore

1945 ends with Bé and Wouter back in Medan, free from the Japanese concentration camp. Bé is receiving correspondence from family in the Netherlands and from POWs that were with Jaap in Burma, and one in particular who was with Jaap when he passed away. Bé now has to figure out life as a widow, with a small child of five years old.

1946

The year starts out with Bé preparing for her return to the Netherlands. This is a country Wouter has never known as home and will be very different from the tropical climate of Sumatra. The letters continue to come from family.

Rotterdam,

Dear Be,

Since contact between us has resumed, I would like to start writing to you again, like we used to, although I have the feeling that you might already be on your way to Holland.

From what we hear here in Holland, staying in Indie may not be a good idea. It seems to be quite peaceful on Sumatra, however, not so much on Java, so we advise you to leave as soon as possible.

To wrote us that the situation over there is a lot worse than we originally heard. With Jaap "gone," now, Dick gone as well, and also Nel, how terrible! It is a blessing for Nel's parents that To regularly visited her and was with her when she died. Bert is now on his way to Holland with her two sons. I wonder if he ever knew his second son who is 3, so it is actually impossible.

From the company, Frese & Hogeweg, we received a request to inform them about Jaap and Dirk, which I did.

Have you heard anything of the other gentlemen of the firm? Please let us know who is still alive.

Bert Bekkenkamp died as well. According to Tante Co from Velp, he was shot to death. His wife, who was in Ambarawa Camp, will soon be on her way to Holland.

Henry van Tol is in Singapore, his wife and daughter were in Tjideng Camp, just like To.

5 January 1946

Because of different circumstances, I had to leave this letter until now. We were busy with Christmas and my birthday, as well as making "condolence visits." To gave us the difficult task of informing Nel's parents of her passing on Dec. 5th, 1944, in Kramat Camp. Apparently, she originally managed to stay out of the camp for some time.

The news regarding Ber, from what we heard from the Red Cross, was always: "missing, missing." As I mentioned, he was on the New Amsterdam, but was "left behind" in Singapore because of health reasons.

In the mean time, we received your letter from Dec. 9 on Dec. 29, after which we received your letter from Dec. 23 on January 4th, just after your parents visited here and stayed the night before going back to Goeree. Opa and Oma v.d. Voort had a lovely time with us. We hope to hear from you soon and that you will get this letter in time before you leave on the Noordam. This week we went on a shopping trip for the boys: the two of Nel's, Woutertje and Dickie. For each of them, we bought 2 pair of stockings, track pants and ordered "interlock" [thick shirts] since we have to wait for the correct sizes. For you, I hope to get some underwear from "Kerckhoven's" and then at "the brothers Coster" we ordered suits and overcoats for the boys. We will make sure that they are all well dressed, and Mams has a lovely coat for you as well, so do not spend too much money on Woutertje as 700 guilders for two meters of white flannel on the black market is terrible. We also paid 650 guilders for a month worth of potatoes and 140 guilders for a kg of sugar, but the price you paid, makes us cry.

The people coming back from Indie are called "Black Pieters" here, although they are more white than those where you are!

Your parents have the guest room ready for you, and we will also always have room for you – a room with running water and enough "coal" for heating.

We will discuss finances at a later date; first you have to arrive here safely.

Your last letter made us smile, as you refer to our conversation in Eindhoven, when you referred to yourself as "the young Mrs. Bebelaar" and to Mams as the "old Mrs. Bebelaar" and now you are teaching Woutertje the difference between parents and grandparents. He will think that we are very old. We very much hope that he will look like his father, as every time we received his letters, we had such a "good feeling" and knew that he was happy. We will talk about this later, and also about Nico and Frans, although their attitude towards us has changed after everything that has happened. Some days we can talk about this, and other days it brings tears to our eyes.

I am sure you are experiencing this as well.

When you come here, the house is the only thing that has remained the same, but the people in it, however, have changed. "Vader" is still Vader, although he is also Grandfather, so young and old. Mams is still the same, but very busy since the office is up and running again, and we have real problems without a housekeeper and maid.

Adrie was married and lives not far from here. Dave is still at home and has the big room downstairs. Gerrit has his own room next to the bathroom, and the other two are still in our room. It is very messy in the cellar, where we store coal, wood, as well as potatoes, cabage and onions.

Now dear Bé, I will end this letter and will have much more to talk about when you get here.

I was very "touched" on my birthday with a gift from Nico and Frans. They presented me with an enlargement of a photo of Woutertje and had it "coloured" and framed. Your parents loved it as well and were very impressed.

So now, many kisses from Gerrit Hans and Jaapje and also for Woutertje, a big kiss from Mams and Vader.

The letter from Rotterdam references David looking like Jaap, and a Jaapjte. David is a younger brother of Jaap, and Jaaptje is a half brother, who has been named for his deceased older brother.

Bennekom, 5 January 1946

Darling Bé,

Yesterday, we came home again to Bennekom. We stayed with Bram and Nel (Risseeuw/Oltmans) for two weeks in Goedereede and celebrated Christmas and New Year there. Nel hopes that in the new year we will all be together again. Except for Jaap. We miss him very much and carry this sadness. On Thursday Jan. 3 we left for Rotterdam and stayed one night with the Bebelaar family. David looks so much like Jaap. Mrs Bebelaar was already busy collecting clothes for little Wouter and also for you. Through his work, Mr. Bebelaar knows many people and can get things. We have to wait and see what we can get using our coupons. I hope you will receive this letter in Port Said. It would be so nice if you could be back here at the end of January. You asked us to sort things out. We think you should first come here to Bennekom to recover from from what you have gone through. And then, later, you can stay with other family. Kor and Nel look forward to having you and spoiling you and so are the Bebelaars. I hope that it will not be so cold when you arrive. It has been very cold, but there is a change in the weather coming. Jantje, from Bram and Nel, is a darling little boy. Iek is a sturdy boy. It was so funny when he asked, "Is auntie Bé negro?" He thinks that everyone in the Indies is black. What a chaotic situation it is in the Indies. Thank heavens that you will soon be home safe. Father already spoke with the coal man to get more coal for the stove, so you will not be cold. We do not know where we can pick you up. The newspaper asked the families not to come to the boat arrival because they will be driven home by car. First they will go to a hotel where the paper work will be done. The weak and the sick will go to care centers. We will wait and hear more later. That you come home is the most important. Heere ordered three packages with food in America. The first package arrived here yesterday: 1 kg cheese, 1 kg butter, 1 kg sausage, 1 kg pork meat in a tin. Heere has been good to us in the war years. And so have Nel and Bram. Good that they have not suffered in the war years, except for the scary times of bombardments. But not like us at the front line. I enjoy the quietness now, not being shot at. And not sitting in the cellar away from the grenades. Our front room is small and cosy. In the back, the windows have been closed shut and covered with planking. But we cannot sit there anyway because we can only heat one room. Next week we will get the upstairs room ready for you and little Wouter. Egbert Krijkke is still in Java and no chance to repatriate soon. Nel Pfeiffer is in Singapore. She had hoped to get on the Nieuw Amsterdam (ship) but that did not work. She is still in Singapore.

Bé, we can now say we will see you soon. Be strong, Bé, be good. Love. Kisses.

Your mother and father.

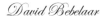

Bennekom, 7 January 1946

Darling Bé,

Father had just posted the previous letter to you when another letter from you, dated 20 December, came. A disappointment that the boat departs later, but it is only 10 days. We wait for further news. Our plan was that we were to stay at Kor's, but now we stay home waiting for news from you. We are happy that your housing is now better. Thank you, Bé, that you will bring coffee and tea. I just made myself a delicious cup of tea, without surrogate! We received a second package from Heere. We will keep it for when you are home. Neeltje Krytte is moving forward. Walking is still not possible; she can barely stand up. She suffered a great deal in the concentration camp. You wrote, Bé, that you had some tins of food. Don't save them up for us if you can use it yourself. The food on board the ship Noordam may not be the best. The food supply here is getting better. I hope you can send us a telegram when you will arrive. For now, bye, bye, Bé. We will see you soon. I can't wait to see my new shoes you are bringing. I only have 1 pair left. Give Wouter Jan a kiss from his grandmother. Love and kisses from your mother.

We also wish you a safe and happy voyage!

The following letter from Sgt. Ras provides some information, the signifigance of which had not been realized at the time. Bé has asked about some of Jaap's belongings, and, in his response, Sgt. Ras provides details of items that Jaap sold to acquire food. And then, one sentence jumps out, which could easily go by unnoticed, regarding the whereabouts of a pen. Sgt. Ras questions whether Jaap lost this item during his trip on the *Van Imhoff*. Unless Jaap had told Ras about the trip, how would anyone think he lost this item there? Based on this letter, it can be assumed that Jaap was aboard the *Van Imhoff* in January 1942, transporting prisoners to India, when it was torpedoed by a Japanese fighter jet.

Singapore January 9th, 1946

Dear Mrs. Bebelaar,

One quick letter after your letter from the fifth of this month. I hope you will receive it in time and that you are not yet on the boat. For the time being we are not yet going to the Netherlands. I still have my work here, and as long as that lasts I am staying here. I will give Hank Moddemeyer the things which I described in my previous letter regarding Jaap's watch that he sold in camp #45 for 110 rupeco. Longines were very much wanted by the Japs; that's why he sold it. I don't know much about his fountain pen, I have never seen it. Did he have it with him? Maybe he lost it on his trip with the Van Imhoff's. It is very sad that Jaap did not get to share a lot of time with Woutertje, about whom he talked often and loved very much. I personally find it very sad that our friendship, which hadn't been that long yet, was very close and had to end the way that it did. Usually friendships, when you are a bit older, are not as deep as when you are young. This friendship was so deep because we knew everything about each other, even how we got to know our spouses. Moreover, both Jaap and I loved music and we therefore had many things in common. He even played the violin, which in these dark days was quite an event. As soon as we get to Holland we will come and see you, I promise. Because, in this case especially, we can't postpone it. Furthermore, I wish you a good trip and a pleasant welcome as well from my wife for you and Woutertje.

Kind regards and let's say see you soon.

Dorus Ras

PS: Received your last two letters very late because you had given me a military rank and they were first sent to Sabang. The last one I just received yesterday

Bé and Wouter are now ready to return to the Netherlands. They are scheduled to leave Sumatra on January 20, 1946, aboard the *Noordam* and return to Amsterdam.

Noordam	20-01-46	Belawan	20-02-46	Amsterdam

Bedelaar—Oltmans, And. F. J., — 21—10—11.— Heidelaan 3, Bennekom.
Bedelaar, Wouter J., x 28—4—40 — idem.

S.S. *Noordam*

Bé is aboard the ship, and letters still keep coming.

Goedereede, 23 Jan. 1946

Darling Bé,

Jantje is having his afternoon nap, Gon is playing outside riding a sleigh in the snow and Iekje is at school. Now I am looking forward to writing you a long letter about this and that. I just put some extra coals on the fire. It is a bit reckless, but I really want to sit warm. I don't like it having it so cold, but what do you do. It was worse last year in the hunger winter. Now at least we are well nourished. I am not complaining. We are so lucky that we survived the war years with the whole family. But I want to give you an idea what to expect when you arrive back in Holland. I still write this letter to the Indies because from the newspapers we gather that your ship has not yet left. In the newspapers, I read that children who have not had the measles are again allowed, next month February, to go on the evacuation ships. (Note: There was an epidemic of measles.) I am really looking forward to this summer when you will be staying with us for a long time. We live so close to the beach. Now that I am sitting here in the cold, it is hard to believe that we will be sitting on the beach this summer in the warm sun. They have cleared a section of the beach, cleared of mines.

In the New Year Bram and I visited Zeeuws-Vlaanderen (Zeeland Flanders). Some people say that the destruction in Z.VI, in the battle for the Scheidt river, is worse than the invasion in France. Towns like Breskens, Oostburg, Sluis destroyed. Groede is the only village that was not bombed. But near Groede, you remember that flat part, there was hand to hand combat. Many of our friends are dead or wounded. Our beloved vet lost his left arm.

The journey from Goedereede to Z. VI was a journey with obstacles. We left Goedereede at 5 in the morning. It was dark and bitterly cold. Bram was dressed for it: two long underpants, woollen stockings, woollen shirt, two sweaters, warm jacket, woollen scarf, ear muffs, hat, a thick winter coat, two pair of mittens, and two spoonfulls of cod liver oil. And your elegant sister in the latest Goereesche Chique: two thick woollen directoires, 2 pair of woollen stockings, 1 pair of woollen socks, 2 woollen undershirts, dress, sweater, long pants, a thick winter coat, a hat, 3 scarfs, warm thick gloves. Try to picture this. This elegant pair. At 6 am the streetcar left for Middelharnis. On 6:25 we got bicycles to cycle to Ooltgens plaat, still pitch black with strong headwinds. On the ferry to Brabant, bicycling to Bergen op Zoom. There the train to Vlissingen. There a small ferry to Breskens Z.VI. We watched the sunset from the ferry. And then finally, we bicycled from Breskens to Groede, to stay with Bram's family there. After two weeks, the return trip. The same route.

Today we got oranges. Delicious. We haven't seen oranges in years. The food supply in the stores is slowly getting back to normal. A few shortages, like butter. But people look healthy. Except the bodies lack color yet. For children's clothing we still make do, mending old clothes. Remember that Iek was 2 years old when the war started and now he is a big boy of 8 and a half. He has two pairs of stockings for which I knitted new feet twice. In the big city, Rotterdam, you see ladies in fur coats but with bare legs. Unbelievable.

What was very special this year is that we had a Christmas tree. I had a few candles. In the morning the church bells called us to church. And in the afternoon, we had the Christmas tree with the candles on and the curtains wide open. Everybody could look inside, and we looked outside. Bé, I hope that this year you and Wouter can celebrate Christmas with us all. As soon as you are here, I will also go to Bennekom. We all arranged that already. I am going to end my letter now. I can write on forever. You have no idea how often I think of you. One of the few words that Jantje can say is Bé. Dear Bé, be good. When you are here we will spoil you and Wouter. Many greetings and kisses for you and Wouter, from your NEL.

Hello darling Woutertje. You will soon be here with your auntie Nel. Iekje and Gon can't wait to see you here. You can play together. Dear darling boy, a kiss from your auntie Nel.

Goedereede, 19 Februari 1946

Dear Bé,

Welcome to Holland. I hope that the Dutch air will help you get strong and healthy and the same for little Wouter. In the last few months, there has not been a day that we didn't think of you. The letters going back and forth. I think in your homecoming to Holland there will be difficult moments. You will miss Jaap, certainly. But looking after the little boy may make it a bit easier. Soon, I hope to meet you. You will always be welcome in Goedereede. And if you think you need my help, you can count on me. For now, I think you should take the time to recover from what you have lived through. This is not the time to make big decisions. Enjoy Holland. Enjoy the family. Also, for my little nephew. Many greetings. Bram

Goedereede, 19 F ebruary 1946

Dear Woutertje,

This book with drawings in pencil is for you. Maybe you can ask Opa to help you. And the postcards, you may play with or cut out what you want. Come with your mama to visit us soon. From your cousin, Gonnie

All the family are anxiously waiting to see Bé and Wouter. These are all new faces for Wouter, and for his little cousins, they also have never met Bé. Nel's husband Bram will be a shoulder for Bé to lean on as she works her way through governmental paperwork, and Bram's role as a Notary Public will be helpful.

Bé now starts the process of re-creating her life. This process takes many avenues, including having to prove she was married.

CIVIL REGISTRY
EINDHOVEN

EXTRACT

From the Civil Registry of the municipality Eindhoven it appears that

on Ten December nineteen hundred and thirty-six

Were married: Jacob Bebelaar

And Oltmans, Andrea Pieternella Johanna

Issued for obtaining of a Military Pension

27 July, 1946

Civil Registrar of Eindhoven

1947

Bé has been busy building a life since her return to the Netherlands. Prior to leaving, she had graduated and worked as a pharmacy assistant. Upon her return, she takes to studies again, and on February 25, 1947, passes the examination in Chiropody, from the First Dutch Acadamy for Chiropody, Beauty, and Body Culture.

September 1947, Bé receives a very special letter from the Queen.

Palace Het Loo, 1, September 1947

Mrs. The widow J. Bebelaar-Oltmans

Heidelaan 3, Bennekom

After the seizure of our territory in the Far East, your husband Jacob, who as a non-commission officer of the Royal Netherlands East Indies Army, participated in the defence of this area, was transported as a Prisoner of War of Japan.

As a result of the unbearable conditions, he died in Burma on June 22, 1943. With feelings of deep sympathy, I offer you, your young son and other family members, my sincere condolences.

May his memory give you strength in the years to come.

Wilhelmina

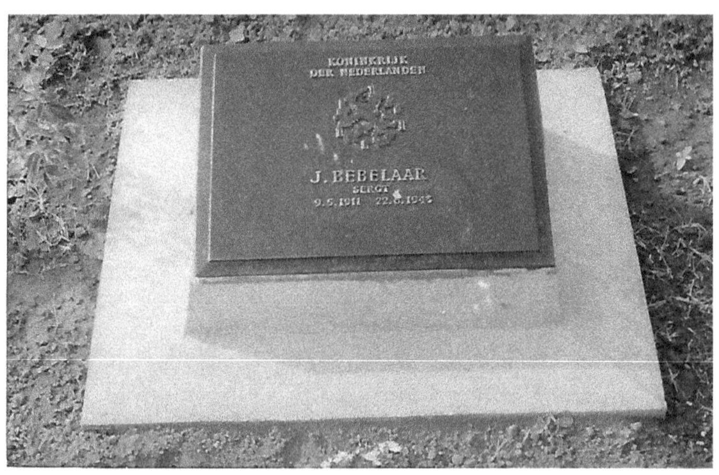

1948

The memories keep coming:

From: Netherlands Red Cross s'Gravenhage, 26 Aug. 1948

To: Mrs A.P.J. Bebelaar - Oltmans

Sarphatipark 71, upstairs

Amsterdam

Re: The late J. Bebelaar

Hereby we send you a package from the Red Cross in Batavia. Inside the package is a spoon that belonged to your husband, the late Jacob Bebelaar.

Please return the signed receipt.

The Department Head, Department A.

The 1950s: More Moving, More Change, More Loss

1950

At the outset of the 1950s, Bé looks to start rebuilding her life and building a life for her son, Wouter. The experiences of the time in the Japanese concentration camps have left Wouter with issues that are beyond the abilities of Bé to deal with. She seeks help to guide him through his issues.

FOUNDATION PSYCHOLOGICAL PAEDAGOGIC
INSTITUTE "AMSTERDAM"
SCHOOL FOR INDIVIDUAL EDUCATION
VAN EEGHENSTRAAT 183
TELEPHONE 23473

JULY 1950.

To the parents or caregivers of our students.

On Monday morning 4 September at 9 o'clock the new course will take place. At the end of the last school year we have been able to deliver several students to various educational institutions in Amsterdam and elsewhere. We hope and expect that they will make good progress at their new school and achieve them and our stated goal.

You have all received the summer reports and we will be happy to talk about it as well after the vacations.

SCHOOL NEEDS. Books and scripts are provided by the school for the Lower Education Department. All students must, however, have a school bag, pencils, flat, drawing box (name and address), a few tubes of paint: yellow, black, red, light blue, white; a pair of brushes; For the elderly: a suitcase and a bottle of O.I ink.

SCHOOL SWIMMING. We want to reiterate on this occasion that only absenteeism is allowed for urgent cases after prior consultation. In case of absence due to illness, please inform this by telephone or by telephone (23473) immediately. When a student returns to school after a sickness case, would you like to write this in writing, orally or by telephone? We expect that you all want to work in the interests of our students to implement these measures.

SCHOOL TIME. From 9 - 12 and from 1 - 3 hours. Wednesday and Saturday noon free

NEW LEARNING LIONS. As far as they come from Amsterdam, the new students will be expected to attend school on Monday 4 September with one of the parents or caregivers. For each, you will receive another postcard at which time.

PHYSICAL EXERCISE. For the gym lessons, all children will need gymnastics shoes and packs. For any swimming swimsuits. All provided with a brand. You will receive further information about the swimming course.

Speaking for the school: Monday afternoon from 3-4 hours.

We wish parents and children a nice summer vacation.

The Head of the School,

A.H. de Jong

This welcome letter is soon followed by two copies of the payment details and rules for the school:

FOUNDATION PSYCHOLOGICAL PAEDAGOGIC INSTITUTE "AMSTERDAM"

Amsterdam, 15 August 1950

Name: Mrs. A.P.J. Bebelaar-Oltmans Address: Kerkstraat 167, 2e, Amsterdam

confirms that I agree with the following conditions, including her son, named Wouter Jan born 28-4-1940 at the request of the undersigned for the course of 1950/1951, is included in the school of the PPIA Foundation and expressly opposes the Foundation to connect for the resulting obligations.

A. The treatment fee amounts to f 400 per annum in ten monthly term (s) of f. 40 in advance payment by deposit or transfer on account of Stichting vij de Twentsche Bank N.V., branch of Baerlestraat, Amsterdam (bank postgiro: 206800, bank city giro: AA 400)

The first term expires on 1 September a.s.

B. The placement is entered into for the entire course year, provided that interim interruption can not take place, except in very special cases, in which the Board of Directors may grant a dispensation.

C. The handling fee does not include the Municipal School Tax, which tax must be paid directly to the Municipality of Recipient upon receipt of the assessment.

D. The use of medicines is allowed only if an express prescription from the attending physician can be submitted.

E. Medical inspection will take place at least once a year, while costs will be borne by the undersigned.

F. The Foundation is not liable for damage or search of clothing and other items.

Bé does not sign or return this consent form. A document, such as this, to send her only son to an Institute, and dated five years to the day the Japanese surrendered, is something she cannot sign. Bé knows Wouter needs help. He has been going through testing to determine the best course of action for him.

G. Van Der Plas Amsterdam, 16, Aug 1950

Medical Doctor

De Lairessestraat 166

Amsterdam

Dear Colleague:

Wouter Jan Bebelaar, aged 10 years, has been in a Japanese concentration camp in Sumatra for 3 ½ years. I know him from there.

His mother is a widow. His father died in the war. She has to work in an office to earn her living expenses. She cannot cope with the upbringing and education of Wouter. The boy is difficult, undisciplined, forceful at times.

Upon advice, I am referring his mother to you to discuss the situation with her and to accept Wouter into treatment as soon as possible. At age 6 Wouter was tested twice at Watering and not long ago at Bladergroen. The latter thinks it necessary to have Wouter enroll at her school. I think it is better to have Wouter at a normal elementary school, with small classes, for instance the Hildebrand School, and under psycho-therapeutic treatment and control.

I hope you can help here.

Yours, very truly

G. van der Plas

Wouter starts the 1950/1951 school year at the Wilhelmina Catharina School in Amsterdam. A cousin of Bé, and her husband, have moved in with Bé and Wouter. Bé is now able to take a vacation, as she has someone to look after her son.

Postcards from Bé

Cannes, September 5, 1950

Dear Wouter, Anneke, Otto and Nel:

It is so nice here. The nature is like out of a fairytale. Everyday sunshine. We already have seen a lot. Today Cannes, and tomorrow by car to the Alps. It is so beautiful here. The travel was very tiring, but we have a nice room and comfortable beds. We sleep very well and are well rested in the morning. We are now sitting close by the sea and getting a sun tan. Later, we go by boat to visit a couple of islands nearby. Bye, Wouter, bye, everyone, a kiss from mamma Bé.

The Alps, September 6, 1950

Dear All:

A beautiful trip today. It is so nice here. How are you Wouter, and how is the school? Is it a nice school? I think it is. Can you ask Anneke to go with her to the train station to pick me up? And then late to bed. Do a little nap in the afternoon. Greetings to everyone and for Wouter a double kiss. Mammie and Bé.

Monaco, September 7, 1950

Dear All:

Today is Thursday. Monaco. This evening we will play in the casino. It is all so nice here. I am sitting at the boulevard and writing to you. Received your letter. Nice that Wouter is so sweet. How is it at shool? Tomorrow we go to the perfume factory. Bye. See you Sunday evening. Bye, Wouter, a kiss from mamma. Bye, all. Bé

1951

As 1951 begins, Wouter continues to attend school in Amsterdam, and Bé is busy with her work.

April brings Wouter's 11th birthday.

Bennekom, April 27, 1951

Dear Wouter:

Oma and Opa wish you a very happy birthday. Congratulations. Your mother will give you your birthday present. We hope you like it.

> *You are doing so well with the boyscouts. That was quite a festive gathering you had. And you had to get up so early in the morning. We think you will be a very good boy scout. It is a pity that Oma and Opa cannot come to visit you in Amsterdam. Oma cannot travel anymore. Dear Wouter, we wish you a happy day on your birthday. Do you write us back? Bye, Wouter, and a big kiss from Oma and Opa*

July 1951, Wouter finishes his year at Wilhelmina Catharina School. Notes in the report card indicate early on that Wouter has to deal with things much better. In March of 1951 there is a notation that Wouter can work better, but not steady. The Final Report: PASSED OVER.

Soon after the school year ends, Wilhelmina Catharina School closes. Wouter now needs to go to a new school. Bé sends Wouter to the Quaker school in Vilsteren. Here he boards at the school and attends from the 1951 to 1953 school years, leaving in 1954.

At age 11, Wouter goes to the Quaker school, where he is boarded. He needs to take care of himself, so Bé drafts a schedule for him to give him guidance as to the proper use of his time.

The colour coding depicts activities:

Grey: Sleep or Rest

Green: Dressing, Undressing or Shower
Red: Eating
Yellow: School
Blue: Break or Free time

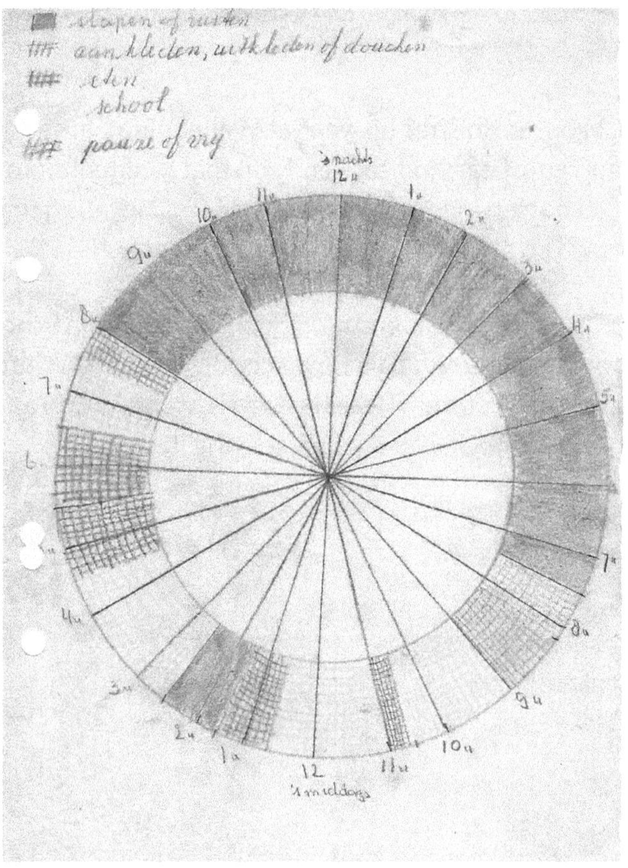

1955

Wouter has now completed his schooling at the Quaker school. Bé is looking for the best opportunities for her and Wouter, now 15 years of age. She starts actions towards a new life. She needs to acquire documentation to support her prior experiences, before her new life can begin.

Departmentment from the Ministery of
EDUCATION, ARTS and SCIENCES
The Hague, 18 February 1955)

THE SECRETARY OF STATE OF MINISTERY OF
EDUCATION, ARTS AND SCIENCES

Declares herewith that from information in the archives of the ministery it is shown that Andrea Pieternella Johanna Oltmans, born 21 October 1911 at Apeldoorn has been examined in the program to obtain a certificate as assistant - pharmacist and has successfully completed said examination and therefore has been issued said Certificate.

For the Secretary of State

The Head of the Department of preparatory

Higher education

(DR. A. J. Piekaar)

To further prepare for her new life, Bé must take care of financial affairs going into the future. She establishes a power of attorney to oversee any future financial dealings.

POWER OF ATTORNEY

The undersigned, Andrea Pieternella Johanna Oltmans, widow of Jacob Bebelaar at Amsterdam, intending to move to Canada, declares herewith for herself and every capacity she may have or acquire that she will give power of attorney to Abraham Adriaan Risseeuw, Notary Public at Goedereede Haven, Noordzijde 30 --------- and in his absence of failure to Ir. Herre Rinia., engineer, living in Eindhoven, Parklaan 24 to represent her in every respect without exception in all matters, relating to personal rights, family rights, business rights, financial affairs, and any other judicial rights.

This power of attorney extends to personal property and real estate, mortgages, payments, tax assessments and any appeals to de made to charges made.

It is all embracing in all judiciary transactions and is given with right of assumption and substitution.

Was signed, March 1955 at Rotterdam,

A.P.J. Bebelaar Oltmans

Arrangements for the journey to Canada continue. One last step is to resign her job:

Ministry of
Social Affairs
and Public Health

31, May 1955
No. 5720

The Minister of Social Affairs and Public Health

DECISION:

his order of 15 March 1955, No. 2368, Personnel Division, to which Mrs A.P.J. Bebelaar-Oltmans counted from 1 March 1955 at her request for a permanent resignation as a writer of A in the National Insurance Bank, which is replaced by "writer A" instead of "writer A" Administrative Officer C 2nd Class.

s'Gravenhage, 31 May 1955
The Minister mentioned,
For this
The Secretary General

M.S. *Prins Frederik Willem*

In the summer of 1955, Bé and Wouter depart the Netherlands for a new life in Canada. They board the Cargo Ship, M.S. *Prins Frederik Willem*. Once in Canada, they make their way to Shanty Bay, Ontario, where Bé will work as the house staff and Wouter will tend to the grounds, for the Angas Family.

While in Shanty Bay, Wouter attends school and works to maintain the property. Bé has some freedom as she has access to a car to complete her duties in looking after the house. They enjoy living on a property on a lake. Water has always been a big part of their life.

Correspondence comes in December from the Dutch government:

Extract of the Registry of Decrees of the Commission A.O.R.

The Hague, 23 December, 1955

In view of the decree of 23 Jan., 1950 Nr. OV.I.II/3547/A

reference the question-list control no. 3547:

considering:

that Jacob BEBELAAR (Netherlander), born at Rotterdam, 9 May, 1911 has died as war victim at Birma on 22 June, 1943;

that on 1 Nov.1955 his descendents are entitled to a payment

Spouse Mrs. Andrea Pieternella Johanna OLTMANS

Child Wouter Jan, born 28 April, 1940

That basis for the calculation amounts to FI. 538;

with attention to art. 21 and 43 of the General War Accident Regulation and art. 1 of the resolution by the Social Ministry

HAS RESOLVED

I. to award, beginning Nov. 1, 1955,

A. Mrs. Andrea Pieternella Johanna BEBELAAR-OLTMANS an amount of FI. 95.12, increased by a cost-of-living-allowance of FI. 27.67 hence a total of FI. 122.79 per month
B. The child Wouter Jan an amount of FI. 53.80, increased with a cost-of-living- allowance of FI. 13.45, hence a total of FI. 67.25 per month

II. To determine that above mentioned PAYMENTS WILL BE PAID TO Mrs. Widow A.P.J. Bebelaar-Oltmans

III. To Mrs. A.P.J. Bebelaar-Oltmans living at c/o Mrs. H. Angas R.R.I Shanty Bay, Ontario Canada to be notified of the above mentioned

a) that the claim to the above mentioned payment under I sub A will lapse on the first of the month following remarriage or death
b) that the claim to the above mentioned payment under I sub B will lapse on the first of the

month folowing the 18th birthday of the child, or was married or died.

c) that she should notify the Commission of a change in her civil status
d) that in the event there is a change in the income of above mentioned entitled, that she should notify the Commission right away. If no notice is received the payments could be reclaimed.
e) that she should notify the Commission of any change in address, or the plan to depart from Canada
f) The fore-mentioned payments will be made monthly by post-cheque after deduction of taxes.

IV According to items (1) and (2) of art. 50 of the general war accident regulation:

(1) Periodical payments under this regulation are indefeasible and cannot be pawned or lent

(2) The mandate to receive these payments can at any time be withdrawn

THE HEAD OF THE Department A.O.R.

1956

Living and working in Canada is hard for Bé. She is lonely and misses her family. She decides that she and Wouter (now called Walter, in Canada) will return to the Netherlands for four weeks to see the family.

To: Mrs. A.P.J. Bebelaar-Oltmans Bennekom, 30 April 1956

c/o Mrs. H.S. Angas

Dear Bé:

This will be the last letter you receive in Canada before you will be leaving by boat to visit us in Holland for 4 weeks. We wish you a bon voyage. We are counting the days. It is still cold here and it is raining. The tulip bulbs are not out yet and that is late. Bye, Bé and Wouter. We will see you soon. Bé, be careful with driving the car. I don't think we can have walks in this weather. Cordial greeting and kisses.

Mother and Father

Opa and Oma.

The voyage begins on Saturday June 2, 1956, aboard the S.S. *Groote Beer*. They depart Montreal for Rotterdam via Southampton and Le Havre.

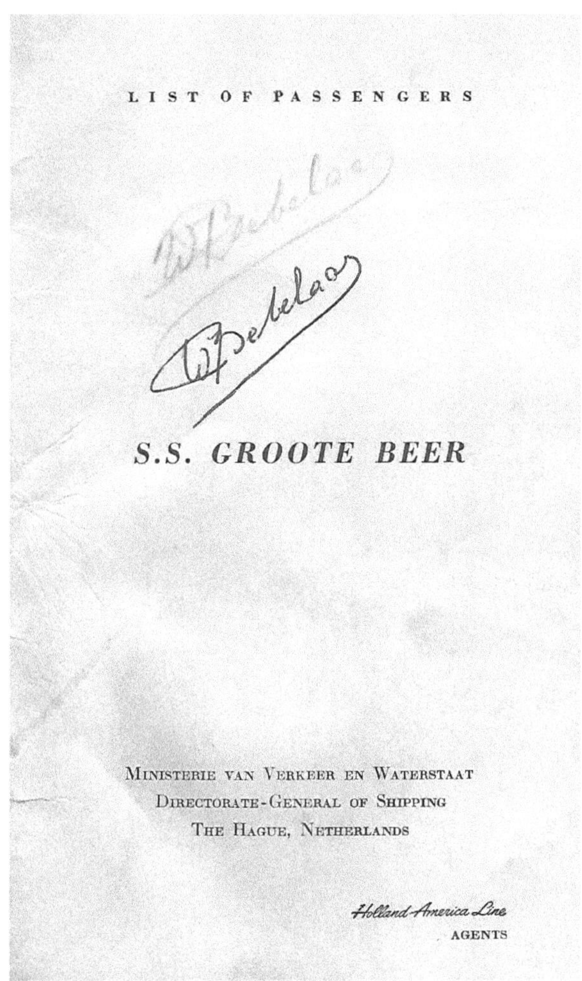
LIST OF PASSENGERS

S.S. GROOTE BEER

MINISTERIE VAN VERKEER EN WATERSTAAT
DIRECTORATE-GENERAL OF SHIPPING
THE HAGUE, NETHERLANDS

Holland-America Line
AGENTS

This is a much different journey for Walter. Coming to Canada on a cargo vessel, there were minimal passengers and no forms of entertainment. This journey is different. An eight-page passenger list means there are a lot of people to meet. A special night is held one week into the voyage on June 9, 1956.

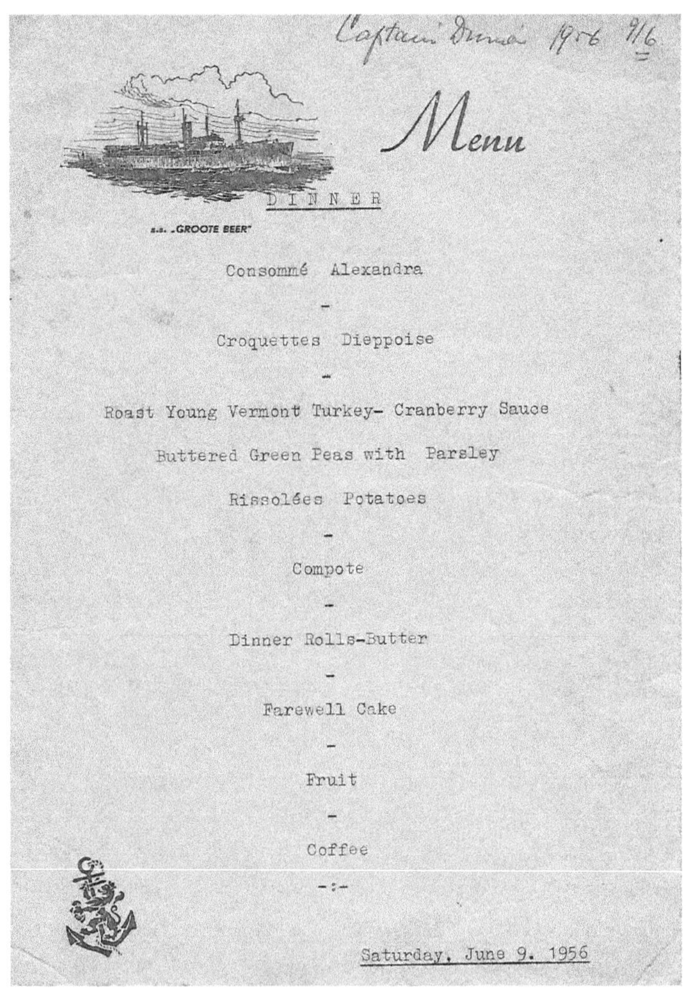
Captain Dinner 1956 9/6

Menu

s.s. "GROOTE BEER"

DINNER

Consommé Alexandra

-

Croquettes Dieppoise

-

Roast Young Vermont Turkey- Cranberry Sauce

Buttered Green Peas with Parsley

Rissolées Potatoes

-

Compote

-

Dinner Rolls-Butter

-

Farewell Cake

-

Fruit

-

Coffee

-:-

Saturday, June 9. 1956

S.S. *Groote Beer*

Bé and Walter arrive back in the Netherlands. It is June 10, 1956. The intended four-week stay is soon to change.

Bé's life has been filled with change: moving to the Dutch East Indies, losing her husband, suffering through the Japanese concentration camps, returning to war-ravaged Holland, dealing with a child who has many effects from the war, and most recently a move to Canada. The next changes for Bé will test her resolve, once again.

July 17, 1956, Bé's beloved father, Jan Jacob Oltmans, passes away at the age of 76.

Heden overleed onze lieve zorgzame Man, Vader, Behuwd- en Grootvader

JAN JACOB OLTMANS

in de ouderdom van 76 jaar.

Bennekom, A. OLTMANS-BÉMOND
Eindhoven, K. A. RINIA-OLTMANS
H. RINIA
Goedereede, N. RISSEEUW-OLTMANS
A. A. RISSEEUW
Hilversum, A. P. J. BEBELAAR-OLTMANS
EN KLEINKINDEREN

Bennekom, 17 Juli 1956
Dorpsstraat 37

Liever geen bezoek

De teraardebestelling zal plaats vinden a.s. Vrijdag 20 Juli des voormiddags 11.30 uur op de Nieuwe Begraafplaats te Bennekom.

Bé and her two sisters, Kor and Nel, grapple with the news and reality that their father has passed away.

August 31, 1956, tragedy strikes again. Alegonde Oltmans-Bemond, Bé's mother, passes away at the age of 78.

Heden overleed onze lieve Moeder, Behuwd- en Grootmoeder

Mevr. Wed. A. OLTMANS-BÉMOND

in de ouderdom van 78 jaar.

Eindhoven: K. A. RINIA-OLTMANS
H. RINIA
Goedereede: N. RISSEEUW-OLTMANS
A. A. RISSEEUW
Arnhem: A. P. J. BEBELAAR-OLTMANS
en kleinkinderen

Arnhem, 31 Augustus 1956

Geen bezoek.

De teraardebestelling zal plaats vinden a.s. Dinsdag 4 September om 11.30 uur op de Nieuwe Begraafplaats vanuit Huize Bethanië, Dorpsstraat 37, Bennekom.

De overledene is opgebaard in de rouwkamer, Spijkerstraat 12 te Arnhem.

Condoleance-adres: Dorpsstraat 37, Bennekom.

This is not the four weeks Bé anticipated when she came back to Holland. She delays her return to Canada, to help her sisters deal with the estate of their parents.

1957

As 1957 begins, Bé makes plans for herself and Wouter to return to Canada. She books passage for the two of them to depart Rotterdam on the *Nieuw-Amsterdam* on April 19. This is a final move, as she makes arrangements to have her belongings, which have been in storage since 1955, accompany her on the journey back to Canada. Bé continues to have to report her income to the Pensions Administration in order to qualify for assistance.

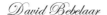

Letter from Institute Administration Indonesian Pensions

To Mrs APJ Bebelaar-Oltmans (April 4, 1957)

No. 3547/BA119/42/1

Re: Payment Mrs. APJ Bebelaar

To Mrs. A.P.J. Bebelaar-Oltmans

Hondecaeter straat 17 (bel)
Amsterdam Zuid

Re your letter of April 2, 1957

In view of your departure to Canada on 19 April 1957 we will next week arrange your payment for the month of April 1957 via a post cheque in your name. Starting with the month of May 1957, as requested by you, the monthly payments will be deposited in your account at the Netherlands Trade Company (Nederlandse Handel Maatschappij) after receipt of your attestation-vita [proof of life]. We include herewith 6 copies of the attestation-vita application form.

You are requested to give us your address in Canada.

In the event that you will start to work in Canada, we require a statement from your employer stating the starting date of your employment and the earnings thereof.

Bé and Wouter depart on the *Nieuw-Amsterdam*, April 19, 1957.

The journey takes them to New York, where they arrive on April 27, 1957, the day before Wouter's 17th birthday.

TREASURY DEPARTMENT
UNITED STATES CUSTOMS SERVICE
UNITED STATES DEPARTMENT OF JUSTICE
Immigration and Naturalization Service

PASSENGER LIST
~~CREW LIST~~
(Cross out one)

Sheet No. 4

44 TRANSIT

Class Tourist 74

CARRIER Netherlands s.s. "Nieuw Amsterdam" 5697 Z Rott 1936
(Nationality, name, and official No. of vessel)

Port of embarkation: Rotterdam

Date of arrival/~~departure~~ April 27th 1957 Port of arrival/~~departure~~ New York, N.Y.

Last foreign port before arrival in United States Southampton April 20th 1957

	(1) NAME IN FULL		(2) Nationality and passport number	(3) CREW		(4) Crew (departing U.S. Flag Vessels only) USCG Z or C.D.B. No. and Name and Address of Next of Kin	(5) This column for use Government officials only (except when carrying certain passengers. See Instructions.)
	Family Name	Given Name and Middle Initial		Position	Where shipped or engaged		
1	ALOP	Else G.	Germany 5712395				C-1
2	AUKEMA	Gerard J.	Netherlands H 650885				C-1
3	BEBELAAR	Andrea P.	Netherlands D 910378				B-2
4	BEBELAAR	Wouter J.	Netherlands E 405725				B-2
5	BROOS	Leuntje C.	Netherlands E 629338				C-1
6	BUURSMA	Menzo	Netherlands H 239369				B-2
7	DE BEER	Martinus J.	Netherlands E 202580				B-2
8	DE JONG	Willem	Netherlands J 012748				C-1
9	DE JONG	Nekeltje	Netherlands J 012745				C-1
10	DE JONG	Bastiaantje	Netherlands J 012746				C-1
11	DE JONG	Teuntje	Netherlands J 012747				C-1

`Bé and Wouter make their way to Toronto. Bé finds work, and Wouter attends school. The battle with the Pension Commission continues.

Institute Administration Indonesian Pensions

To: Mrs. AP.J. Bebelaar-Oltmans

11 Keystone Ave. Toronto Canada

The Hague, 20 November, 1957

The payment that was assigned to you under The General War Accident Arrangement have been reviewed in view of art. 42 of said arrangement. As a result of this review and considering that you are receiving income from work performed our payment to you will be ended as of 1 June, 1957.

The payment for your child Wouter Jan will remain unchanged and is based on the amount mentioned in the enclosed Extract of Decree. Please especially take note of sub d.

Your payment for May 1957, as well as that for your son up to Nov. 1957, and also your payments up to Sep.1, 1956, to which you are entitled, will be transferred to your account with the Nederlandse Handel Maatschappij in Amsterdam.

Bé replies to this notification:

Letter from A.P.J. Bebelaar-Oltmans to Institute for Indonesian Pension Administration (17 December 1957)

In reply to your letter of Nov.20, 1957 no. *3547C/17/218/37*

To my great surprise, I received your message of Nov. 20 that my A.O.O.R. payment has been cancelled in view of my income. However, I would like to give you some further pertinent information about my position.

My earnings here in Canada, about $220 per month are not higher than my last income in Holland. But I assume that you calculate that at the current high exchange rate for the dollar. $220 would convert to FI.880 which is indeed a high income for Holland. But $1 in Canada does not have the same purchasing value as FI4 in Holland. If this were the case, I would not bother you, requesting any payment because the money I receive in Holland is just a small amount converted in dollars. My monthly expenses (for myself and my son) are as follows:

Rent (low for Canada)	$ 70.-	FI. 280.-
food	$ 70.-	FI. 280.-
health and life insuranc	$ 10.-	FI 40.-
transportation expenses	$25.-	FI.100.-
pocket money	$33.-	FI132.-
education	$12.-	FI 48.-
Total	$220.-	FI.880.-

As you can see, I have not yet allowed anything for taxes, utilities, clothing and entertainment. At the moment, we live together in a small house owned by a family but have to move presently as the owner is selling the house. Rentals for small homes are currently in the order of $100 to $125 per month. You could verify this with somebody who is familiar with Canadian prices.

I do hope that you will reconsider your conclusion and reinstate the payment, for which I will be most grateful.

Yours sincerely,

A. P.J. Bebelaar -Oltmans

1958

A new year, but the struggles continue for Bé. She is trying to start a life on her own with her son, Wouter, who is now going by the name Walter, as it is more North-American sounding. Financial struggles continue for them both. Bé is an educated lady, having graduated as a pharmacy assistant, and later studying chiropody. Jobs she is able to obtain in Toronto are administrative in nature with a lower level of pay.

She receives a reply to her December letter regarding the Indonesian Pension funds:

Administration Fund Indonesian Pensions A.O.R. Dept.

Mrs A.P. J. Bebelaar-Oltmans
11 Keystone Ave

Toronto Canada

No 3547/31/42/38
Att. -

Subject: Income from work The Hague, 6 January 1958

In response to your letter of 17 December 1957 I am sorry to let you know that through moneys received of work outside of the Netherlands your eligibility to receive benefits under the A. O. R. were terminated.

Administration Fund Indonesian Pensions
The acting Head of Dept A.O.R.

September 20, 1958, Bé issues her response:

Dear Sir,

In your letter of 6 January 1958, you mentioned: "due to moneys received from work outside of the Netherlands, my A.O.R. payments has been terminated."

The last decision is dated 23 December 1955 and was sent to me while I was in Canada and herein was stated that the decision will be terminated once re-married or after death (Sub I-A and III-a). After I was back in Holland the full amount was paid out to me for the period I was in Canada. I was in Holland for a few months and left for Canada (Toronto) again in April. Before I left, I went to your office and I was given a number of forms to fill out to prove I was still alive in order to be eligible for a benefit. Isn't it normal to go to Canada to work and earn money? And so, it is strange that this was not mentioned to me. Moreover, you mentioned in your letter dated 4 April 1957 that I had to sent the Attestation of Vita back to you in order to get a benefit. I ask you please to take up my case.

The last full benefit I received was until April 1957 (including April). My son, Wouter Jan, was 18 years old on 28 April, and according to the rules his benefit ended starting 1 May 1958.

Attached I send you my Attestation Vita, and of my son I ask you please the moneys that we should receive to put in my account of the Nederlandse Handelsmaatschappij, Vijzelstraat in Amsterdam.

1959

The stress of the battle to support herself and Walter, and the struggles to get the pension funds from the Dutch government, which were promised to her in 1955, start to take its toll. After surviving POW camps and the atrocities she witnessed, and the never-ending battles to carve out a life, Bé reaches a point where she is having trouble coping. Her physician prescribes Stelazine for her, on Mar 31, 1959. This ```(such as schizophrenia, psychotic disorders). Stelazine helps you to think more clearly, feel less nervous, and take part in everyday life. It can reduce aggressive behavior and the desire to hurt yourself/others. It may also help to decrease hallucinations (i.e., hearing/seeing things that are not there). Stelazine is a psychiatric medication that belongs to the class of drugs called phenothiazine antipsychotics. It works by helping to restore the balance of certain natural substances in the brain.

Bé continues in her job with the YWCA in Toronto. She receives a review of her performance, in which she expresses some concerns regarding the security of her position due to changes coming to the YWCA organization.

COUNSELLING DEPARTMENT EVALUATION

May 25, 1959

Supervisee: Andrea Bebelaar

Supervisor: Elizabeth Macmillan.

This past year has seen Mrs. B. not only develop well in her capacity as Rooms Registry interviewer, but also accept suddenly and heavily, increased responsibility as the sole Rooms Registry worker due to the lengthy illness of the registry supervisor. Mrs. B. accepted this capably and graciously.

As Rooms Registry applications declined in the early months of 1959, Mrs. B. found herself able to assume stenographic work for other Metropolitan staff members. She did so eagerly and through this has not only become better acquainted with the staff concerned, but also with the various aspects of the total association. This is particularly helpful in view of her keen interest in the YWCA.

As the Rooms Registry approaches hourly and geographic change, Mrs. B. has expressed concern about her own position. However, it is hoped that her commercial skills as well as those in the Rooms Registry work, will be utilized by the YWCA.

While Mrs. B. is capable of independent responsibility, it is suggested that she be given help and support through this time of change.

The 1960s: The Family Dynamic Changes

1961

June of 1961 sees a change in the family dynamic. Walter marries on June 24. He is now balancing the needs of his wife and his mother, and is no longer under his mother's roof. He has found work in the shipping industry.

December 1961, Bé gives Walter a photo album for Christmas. The album is titled, **THIS IS YOUR LIFE, 28-4-40 TO 24-6-61.** She has a note on the first page: For Wouter, As a Reminder of the years with your mother. Dec 25, 1961.

1962

Bé makes a return trip to the Netherlands in June 1962. She spends time with family and old friends and reaches out to contacts she had from her time in the Dutch East Indies. Once home, she receives a letter from one of the ladies she had sent flowers to while in Holland.

The Hague, 4 Sept. 1962

Thank you very much for the flowers. First of all, that you were thinking of me and secondly because I love flowers. I put them next to the portrait of my husband. When one is alone in this world it is heartwarming to receive a sign of companionship. You know that,

too. And you have a son. You can be relaxed that the grave is cared for. It is beautiful there. One cannot find a better place. If your son visits it, I hope he will write me about it. The trip there is not easy. Thanbuzayat is a remote place. But your son will find a way.

Again, many thanks and my apology for writing so late. I was away. I was traveling for the Foundation and also for my own pleasure. Did you ask about my age? The Director of the Foundation has given it to you already. I am 59. Still young, otherwise I would not be able to travel so much and do so much work for the Foundation. Best wishes and cordial greetings.

Yours

From:

Mrs van Anrooy
32 Parkflat

The Hague, Holland

Bé continues her efforts to lobby the Dutch government for the reinstatement of the financial support that was promised to her as a war victim.

Toronto, 15 Sep. 1962

The Right Honourable H. Fock

Private Secretary of H.R.H. Prince of the Netherlands
Soestdijk

Dear Mr. Fock,

Since I have had difficulties for a long time, relating to payments under A.O.R. (General War Accidents Pension) and it has been impossible to get cooperation from the Institute Administration Indonesian Pensions who is charged with this, I requested an audience with H.R.H. via Mrs. V.d. Kaaden, Rotterdam. A few days before my departure for Holland, where I will spend time with my family, I was notified that the request could not be granted. I would like to explain in writing what my difficulties are.

To start with I want to mention that during the 2nd World War I was in Japanese prison camps in Sumatra for 4 years and returned to Holland in February 1946 as a widow. My husband had been a prisoner of war and died at the Burma Railroad. My only son was then 6 years old.

Soon after my return a financial arrangement was made for remaining widows and children. This has been a great help during the years in Holland and the education of my son. I had no pension, or any savings, as we only had been married for a few years when war broke out. I only had a small life insurance payment.

Since my son is not a studying type and it is impossible to find jobs in Holland without a diploma, I decided to immigrate to Canada in 1955. In 1956 we visited Holland for a short while and returned to Canada in 1957.

Before my return to Canada I discussed everything with the Institute Administration War Pensions (Neuhuyskade The Hague) and received a number of forms which, after signature by the Dutch Consulate I had to return so that the payments could continue. After the first return I was notified that the payments could no longer be made because I had "a too-high income." I had a job as interviewer at the YMCA for $50 per week. As I did not agree with the Commissions decision a long correspondence followed (enclosed here with) I could not convince the Commission that this income could not be compared with the last income in Holland when I worked at the Medical Department of the Government

Insurance Bank (Amsterdam) and then did receive the Indonesian compensation payment.

I would like to give you some reasons why I believe to be unfairly treated in the hope that you can mediate in this.

When, after having been in Holland for some time, and recovered from the misery and hunger I had experienced during 4 years of Japanese prison camp, I felt it my duty to start working again, since I was healthy and, with the help of the A.O.R. payment, I could support myself and my child. I never took advantage of the highest payment that many people received with the recommendation of an old family doctor who would declare that the person was not able to work anymore after the camp experience. Furthermore, I knew several people who gave illegal information, e.g. not being married while in fact they were. For these people it meant a double income.

I do understand that it is difficult for the Institute to verify and check all the applications, but I am personally embittered that this small payment is refused, while I as a single woman try to support myself and my child by hard work.

At present I work for an affiliate of the Major Insurance Company of 1845, but at a much lower salary than I made before at the YMCA.

In all probability my Canadian income is assessed on the basis of the exchange rate of the dollar (which is high) and not on its purchase value. The Canadian standard of living compares to 2 guilders in Holland and not to the exchange rate of 4 guilders per dollar. House rents are very high compared to salaries; my monthly expenses (rent, utilities, etc.) are more than $100. I now live in part of a house at $ 70 per month but have to find another address because the house is being sold.

Lowest rents are $90- $100 plus extra costs. Although one is partly insured against medical expenses, there will always be uninsured costs. Life in Canada is not cheap.

Enclosed salary notices show that after deducting tax, insurance premiums, etc. I net about $200 per month, which is hardly enough to make ends meet. I therefore cannot agree with "too high income" given as the reason to stop my A.O.R. payments.

While I dislike having to bother you with these complaints, I hope that you can understand that I feel unfairly treated. I always thought that these compensation payments were instituted as an accommodation for widows of prisoners of war during the 2nd World War, who lost their lives for their fatherland.

It is my hope that through your intermediary the A.O.R. payment can be re-instituted retroactively.

Most grateful for your cooperation in this, I am

Most sincerely

A.P.J. Bebelaar-Oltmans

Bé receives correspondence, dated October 10, 1962, confirming receipt of her letter by the Prince. Subsequent to that confirmation, she receives the following notification:

HRH Prince of the Netherlands Soestdikj Palace 22, October 1962

At the order of H.R.H Prince of the Netherlands, I am informing you that I brought your request of 15 Sept. 1962 to the attention of the Institute Administration Indonesian Pensions, Neuheuyskade 32, The Hague.

Unfortunately, this did not ensue in a revision of the decision, which you deemed unfair. Their reaction was given to me as follows:

"The income of the subject person in Canadian dollars was according to stated regulations converted at the current exchange rate in Dutch valuation. It is not allowed to deviate from this regulation, even at the circumstances stated by the subject person. This decision also holds for other foreign concerned parties."

Considering that taking these foreign payments into account it seems to me infeasible to convert them other than according to the official exchange rate. Every other norm would be subject to greater subjectivity.

Your request reminds me that the given regulation is not ideal, but this is often the case with other events in life.

I hereby return the attachments you included with your letter of Sep.15.

The Acting Private Secretary of HRH Prince of the Netherlands

This effectively ends the chances of Bé receiving the support she believes she is entitled to based on previous documents issued to her. She must now focus on moving forward with her life in Canada and continue to endure her financial struggles.

1963

In 1963, there is once again changes in Bé's life. In June, she is presented with a grandson. This is a very happy occasion for Bé, for now she is OMA.

A letter that Bé issued in October 1963 seems to indicate that she has made arrangements to cash–in a life insurance policy. It also indicates that she is ill.

Sent by: Mrs. A.P.J. Bebelaar-Oltmans, Toronto

Dear Sir,

The insurance company, Amstlven, wrote me April 26, 1963 that the last payment from my insurance was deposited in my bank account with the Twentsche Bank in Rotterdam. I opened this account on 25-6-1962, account number 15.0800, with a deposit of fl 7000. At that time, I was in Holland on leave. Have you received the deposit from Amstleven?

Because of illness I was not able to write you earlier. It is very likely that I will be purchasing a house, and I will need the money for a down payment. What would be the total amount?

Could you tell me what the easiest way is to transfer this money to Canada? What is the amount in Canadian dollars? What is the current exchange rate?

I hope to hear from you.

Yours truly,

Mrs. A.P.J. Bebelaar-Oltmans

The following month brings the response from the bank:

Rotterdam, November 18, 1963

Mrs.A.P.J. Bebelaar-Oltmans,
34 Woodlavvn Ave., West,
Toronto, Ontario, Canada

Mrs,

Your limited deposit account No.15-0800g

In response to your letter of 12 October, we will send you one duplicate copy of your account from the opening until the present, to which we have included a short statement for each posted post.

The notes, to which the items relate, we have pursuant to your instruction sent to Ms J.M. Bergkamp-Radstaake, Vondellaan 65, Arnhem. We have the mail and the notes are still under her designation.

The cheapest way to transfer the credit to your account to Canada is through a transfer to a bank account by you giving banking institution information in Toronto.

FIs.9,453.13 - balance as of now
"233.19 - interest to date
FI. 9,686.32

FIs4.84 - ½ % provision ovr FIs.9,686.32
5 34 "° 50 - airmail costs
Fis.9.680,98 a 3.34 3/8 is Can ~ $ 2,895.25

According to the provisions in force for limited deposit accounts, you can withdraw amounts to FIs.500 per calendar month without prior ongoing cancellations are requested up to a maximum of FIs.1,000 total, per calendar month while for requests above the previous ones mentioned amounts ~~ one month cancellation is required. As seen, if you request the entire balance of your depositing account, we will pay the balance from your account as stated on December 18, 1963, so that you will be entitled to the balance plus interest on that date arranged.

We gladly welcome your messages,

Yours sincerely,

THE TWENTSCH 'BANK N. V'

At the end of 1963, correspondence by Bé once again makes reference to an illness she endured earlier in the year.

December 27, 1963

Due to a long stay in the hospital at the beginning of 1963 and after that not having been able to drive for some time, I neglected to take out my 1963 driving license.

I would appreciate if you kindly would supply me with the driving license for 1963, to be able to apply for the 1964 license.

Enclosed you will find my driving license for 1962-No. 287140.

Thanking you for your cooperation,

Yours very truly,

1964

September 1964 brings news of the passing of David Bebelaar on September 24. He was 77 years old. This is a further blow for Bé and Walter, as this was Jaap's father. He was Bé's father-in-law and Walter's grandfather.

1965

May 1965 is the first communication with friends and family since 1963.

Rijswijk, 7 May 1965.

Dear Be,

Why did we not hear from you for such a long time? We hope you are not sick or are have other problems? Usually I receive a letter for my birthday (March 26) and this time we also did not hear from you. We hope there is not a serious reason for you not writing? Ees and I are mostly in Apeldoom now. Hans and Nelleke are separated now and how much longer we stay there, no idea. Hans has his school in Apeldoom and so Nelleke now is staying with her sister in The Hague. How this will end we have no idea and probably a cool down period is sometimes a good thing. They might learn from this: when two fight both are are at fault. Nelleke has strong guilt feelings. Hans has changed a lot, Bé. There is not much left of this normally very happy person. This February they celebrated their 11 wedding anniversary.

In Bussum all is running smoothly. Anneke was in hospital for a week. She had a D and C done, and this procedure has done her a lot of good, and she is very busy now with her 4 kids. She does a lot of sewing and knitting. We do not worry about Otto and her. We both are okay, too. In Apeldoom it is a bit hectic, more than here. On Liberation Day, Hans has taken us over to our spot here and this weekend we are going to Apeldoom again for a few weeks. I needed to be back here for my anticoagulation treatments and my diabetes check up.

Is Wouter okay and also Shirley and the little David? Is he walking by now already? Do you visit them regularly?

Spring here is terrible. Rain every day and wind. We do not see the sun. Ees can't stand this. It does not bother me. I am not allowed to sit in the sun, anyway. But with a little sunshine the world will look more pleasant. And how is Nenne now? Has she improved a bit by now or will her situation not improve anymore? Do you still stay in contact with Rita? If so, please give her my best regards.

We worry a lot about the situation Hans and Nelleke and how this will end; we have no idea at all. They have not filed for divorce yet. Bé, this marriage was never very good, but I notice that they still love each other. A reunion was organized again in the Kurhaus, but we did not go this year. This time not a very long letter, Beetje, but if you write us soon we know that all is well with you and I will treat you to a very long, informative letter.

Love and all the best also for your grandson and children and for you a big kiss,

Jo and Ees.

A second letter received in September is full of news regarding the on-goings of friends and their families.

Mrs Bebelaar

70 Delisle Ave # 614
Toronto 7, Ontario
Canada

Dear Bé, *Bussum Sept. 16, 1965*

You will be surprised receiving a letter from me. It is long ago that I wrote. We think about you constantly, but this family is so busy. Otto always says, "I write the whole day in the office," thus I cannot count on him to write you.

You probably already know that mother is in the hospital, but now in Bussum. Father and mother (for the kids opa and oma) were in Bussum one day and the next day she was in the hospital. She had breathing difficulties and could not sleep. First she thought she had bronchitus. She asked the doctor, who came for Irene, who had a minor case of pneumonia, to also listen to her lungs. It was not bronchitis, but he wanted her to go to the hospital to do an electrocardiogram. Oma was so scared that she could not breathe, but she calmed down when they gave her injections and oxygen. She has a little heart problem. She needs to rest for 1 month. We do our best to change her mood when she is down. She cannot give up. Opa is staying with us. He is helping out with doing the dishes and the-vacuuming.

We told oma not to worry about Hans. He has to make a decision about him and Nelleke. Nelleke agreed to separate, but we think it should be a divorce. Nelleke still brings her problems to him. For instance, she needs to find another place to stay. Hans has met another woman he is in love with. We've already known her for a couple of years. She is very sweet. She is one of his students. She is originally from Egypt. She is also very sweet to mom and dad (opa and oma). She visits mom to wash her hair, do shopping and so on. We hope that the two will marry and have a happy life together. Hans is still young.

Now, I have to ask how you are doing? Have you had your vacation yet? How is Wouter and his wife Shirley and their son? The little one is already two, isn't it? Time flies. Our Barbara will be 7 this month. Already in grade 2 at school. Irene is in grade 5. She is also growing up. We have had the flu. Opa and I were not ill. But the others were not that lucky. Otto and Joke were ill in bed at the same time.

Dear Bé, now you know how things are going with us. If you have time, mother would be very happy with a letter from you. The examinations and medications are difficult for her. We hope she will get better and be with us for some more years.

This is it for today.

Cordial greetings, also for Wouter and Shirley and love from opa and oma and myself. Anneke

1966

A new year, but the same old battles. Bé, once again takes up the fight to receive the pension money she has previously been denied.

Institute Administration Indonesian Pensions

4 May 1966

To Mrs. A.P.J. Bebelaar-Oltmans

70 Delisle Ave. Apt. 614
Toronto (ON) Canada

With reference to your letter of 25 April 1966 we inform you that according to our letter of 11 February 1960 (no. *3547/0v/5/111/23)* you are not entitled to an AOR-payment in view of the application of anti-accumulation regulations to your extra-income (labour), hence, not because of your Dutch citizenship or that you have not remarried.

In answer to your question about the amount of payment you might expect under the War Accident Regulation I include herewith an information form. I urge you to read this very accurately and after filling it, return it as soon as possible. Please pay special attention to the directions given in the form.

I remark hereby that on eventual return to Netherlands your bruto AOR payment, including all supplements would amount to FI 427.01, irrespective of deduction of income tax, AOW premium or anti-accumulation deduction.

Institute Administration Indonesian Pensions

Deputy Head Dept. A. O. R. W.A. Kuiperi)

Family members start writing to Walter, as they are concerned about Bé. Word has made it back to Holland that she is sick. Walter is now 26, with a wife and son.

Goedereede, 14 July 1966

Dear Wouter

It has been a long time since we last wrote. First of all, how are you Wouter, and how are your wife Shirley and your little son? Recently your mother sent me a photo of the little one. What a sweet child. Especially when they start to walk and talk they are such a delight.

Wouter, Wouter, you live so far from us. We haven't even met Shirley, yet. I miss you all. I hope you can read my writing. My right hand is not so good anymore. Wouter, we heard from Rita ten Bruggenkate that your mother is not well. We were afraid of that because she was so down and sad in her last letter. Rita wrote that she cannot be at the office for more than half a day. And Rita will soon be married. She won't be able to do so much for your mother then. Dear Wouter, can you write us how your mother is and what the doctor says? Your mother wrote that she would like to visit us in Holland, but I don't think she can do it. It is very expensive here. And what if she becomes ill? We would like to see her so much and take care of her. She has had so much sorrow in her life. But this is not possible. We discussed it with aunt Kor from Herre, Bram and I. Don't tell her this. Could you write us soon? We are so worried about our youngest sister.

I don't know your address and send this letter to Rita. She will give it to you.
Dear Wouter, cordial greetings to you, also to Shirley and your son.
AuntNel

Nel, Bé's middle sister, follows up with another letter, a few weeks later.

Goederede, 9 August 1966.

I could not read your address. Please write this in legible print.

Dear Wouter,

Lots of thanks for your very quick reply. We enjoyed such an informative letter. We should write each other a little more because one can lose one another so quickly. But I know one can always have good intentions. Amazing that you can still write in Dutch so well. I can speak English a bit, but to write in English I find a bit difficult. How is your mother? I have not heard from her. I understand writing is not easy when one is in bed. I have the feeling that she is not doing too well, and if the cancer spreads I don't think there is probably much hope, but with the medical knowledge of today who knows. Wouter, we keep thinking of her and it is so sad we cannot just come to Canada to comfort her. She is our youngest sister. Dear boy, please write us again soon. You have never seen how splendid we live here. We have a very comfortable bungalow with big windows and a large patio where we live most of the time. We get the sun in the house all day. The house is built on the border of the village and so we have a splendid view on the seawall. Where you all went swimming, remember? Ger lives here in the village, as you know. He bought a new car, but he does not have it yet and so they stayed home. Just as well since it has been raining all summer. People who went camping returned home.

Your little Dave is already growing up so fast. Quite a handful for Shirley I am sure—what a beautiful name by the way.

Please Wouter, write us soon how your mother is doing.

Lots and lots of greetings for you three from all of us and for the three of you a big kiss from your,

Tante Nel

Word of Bé's illness has spread from family to friends and acquaintances. She receives countless letters of support. Letters are now addressed to Bé at her hospital room: room 344, St. Michaels Hospital in Toronto.

Vroomshoop 25 Aug '66

Dear Mrs Bebelaar,

You might find it strange that I am writing to you since I do not really know you, and I know you only from the reception in Toronto where I met you. Yet – I heard a few things about you – I have always had an interest in you. Now that I have heard about your illness, I just wanted to write to you. Not as a cheap compassion because that would be a bit strange to show that, and that is a bit painful. I write to you to show I am thinking of you.

If I imagine your life, you must have fought against loneliness and disillusionment. I have no idea how you can assess your life in the end. Many things might have made you callous, but I am sure there have been things and feelings that have contributed to your life to make it better. And yet I understand that life is not easy for you and that life might have made you callous and angry when you think of your illness and your future.

I heard from my husband that you are not a 'Christian' in the usual sense of the word. You might think that I am a freak. Really, I am not and yet I would like to ask you not to ban God out of your life and your eventual death. Personally, I have experienced how strong God leads one's life and I have also experienced God's love, the love of a godly father, the love Jesus wanted to give us.

You might think that it is easy to talk this way. You went away to find happiness. That is true, and yet – love here on Earth is so fragile. One often meets with difficult circumstances in life. I have met with them, too. Do you know.that my husband has been praying for you? I think he would never tell you he did, but I think it will be good to let you know that there are people, sometimes far away, who think of you. Mrs Bebelaar, I hope things will work out for you for the best. I wish you a lot of strength, and I hope you will experience God's love. If you can, please write to us, we would appreciate this.

We two have a good life and are happy together. This week the family Brombacher was here. We are in contact with Canada every time again, in particular with the kids, of course.

Best regards from,

M. Brouwer-Diek

Vroomshoop, 25 Aug. 1966

Dear Mrs Bebelaar,

We have not heard from you for a long time and we conclude that you are not doing so well since it is not your habit not to write if you could. When we wrote a letter to Canada we asked after you and your situation and we were told you were in the hospital again, since 14 July.

We can imagine what that means for you because you have many memories that were very painful for you and still are. We of course do not know how the situation is, but we think it must not be too easy because we know the past. You also know we had problems of that sort, too. And so, we should not pretend nothing is going on. That will not be helpful. You know miracles still happen and one can get well all of a sudden, but we also know that sometimes a life will be the sacrifice. We don't know what will happen in your case and you yourself also not. We hope you will get out of this crisis again and that you can go home again and to your job and that you become well again for your children, also. The opposite can also be the case and that you are not allowed to be well again. That is very often the case, isn't it? You know that as well as we do. And if it is the time for you to go it will be – in those difficult circumstances – very peaceful for you if you could believe that there was someone who will give you peace the moment you close your eyes. In no way do I like to 'preach' to you. We have talked about this together at the time. Not enough though, I know that, but I would like to remind you of those moments. You should go and talk with a minister, and that will make the situation much easier for you.

We would love to come and visit you. I told my wife about you. She, too, would love to meet you one day. If we are still well enough in 1967 we hope to come over and visit you. That is what we intend to do. Let us hope so.

We received a very happy letter from Rita, and she wrote about her plans. According to what she wrote they will get married this year. What a surprise. She also wrote she is not working at Comm. Life anymore. The way she left there is very odd. She was so good.

We had Mr and Mrs Brombacher here last week. They wrote us in May they wanted to visit us and that they would stay in Hardenberg and visit us from there, and so they did. And it was very pleasant. Woutje and Dick had grown up to be very nice rascals, actually very nice boys. They themselves were well. Mrs B. misses Canada a lot in many ways. Mr B. not so much because he has a very interesting position, and he loves it. They also had not heard much from Canada. Only from Clamke.

We are doing very well. We are both very happy. So happy we were able to take this step. A few days ago, one of our sons-in-law was over for a few weeks. One of the girls hopes to come to us in October, November and around Christmas – the oldest son and his wife. That will be wonderful. Our wish is that they all would come and live here, but alas ...

I think I will end this letter, and we hope that you are okay and that we will hear from you one of these days. If you, for some reason, cannot write to us, please ask your son to write us. Be sure we did not forget you at all.

Best regards,

your J. Brouwer-Diek

Amsterdam 28 Aug. 1966

Mrs. A.P.J Bebelaar
St. Michael's hospital

Room 344

Toronto, Ont.

Canada

Dear Bé

We heard from Guusje that you are in the hospital. I know that when you are in a hospital you love to receive mail. So here is my letter. I was visiting Kath and she will also write you. How are you, Bé? When you are better, come and visit us in Holland. You can stay with us as long as you like. And how are Wouter and the little David? Have you received my letter, an answer to your letter?

Guusje and the children were visiting you. I am so happy that she does that.

Eddy has his birthday tomorrow and we will have dinner with them. He will be 25. He is a good father to his children. He works at a service station in Fiat. He is a hard worker. He is also very sweet *and good for us. As his mother I feel proud. How is Wouter? Is he better now?*

You probably know that Rosemary has a baby of 1 month. Her husband is from Morocco. They live in Algiers. Anita has not spoken with her parents for two years. Kath and Lex are very sad about it. Maybe Anita will write you about it.

Have you seen Pamela and Patricia? Don't you think that they are tall already? Eddy's children are also very nice, especially Linda. She is the youngest. But we have to keep an eye on her. We were at the Bijenkorf and she tried to run away.

I am still waiting for my driver's test. I applied for it 6 weeks ago. I love driving. Even in the busy streets of Amsterdam, I feel confident. Last week, my instructor had me drive to Rotterdam on the highways and through the city. We left in the evening at 7 and we were back at a quarter past 9. I am taking many lessons so that it becomes routine.

Two weeks ago, Nico turned 70 years old. We had dinner with all the children in a restaurant, and after that we went to a Snip and Snap revue. It was so nice.

Dear Bé, so far today. Cordial greetings from me and Nico. Greetings to Wouter and his wife. A kiss for your grandson. Love. Strength.

From:

Family N. de Leeuw –Waaker

September 1966, Bé is released from hospital but is in no shape to take care of herself. Walter is busy supporting a wife and son, so it is not best for her to come live with Walter. Bé's niece, Janneke, now lives in Montreal with her husband and children. Janneke was always a favoured niece. She agrees to have Tante Bé come and stay with them. She hopes that her mother, Kor, Bé's eldest sister, will come to Montreal to help care for Bé. Janneke is shocked when her mother declines to come help, due to conflicts with social engagements that she will be attending. Janneke takes on the task of caring for Bé on her own.

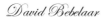

After Bé has been with Janneke and Harry for a short period, they write to Walter to plan for discussions of some hard issues.

Beaconsfield, Sept 24, 1966

Dear Shirley & Walter,

Although you will probably be here with us two weeks from now, it is perhaps better that I write you now so that you can already find some of the answers to the questions that we will be discussing regarding your mother. Your mother is very ill indeed, and we may as well face the fact that she will never again be able to live her own life, without constant care and attention. We don't believe that she can go back to work or even live in her own apartment. Somebody will have to take care of her all the time.

This therefore means that she must stay either with you or us, or in a hospital or nursing home. We must therefore find a solution to this problem when you come here, and this will depend upon what the doctors say after her October 14 check-up, the costs involved and how much of this the insurance will pay. You see, your mother gets more and more pain and she can hardly move or get up out of her bed because of that. We therefore have to give her more drugs, but then her mind gets all mixed up. Things are getting worse, and I don't yet know how she will go back to Toronto next month. But that, we'll see, when it is that far.

The best solution, perhaps, would be if your mother could go to a hospital or nursing home, but the question is whether they will take a terminal case. Anyway, perhaps you can find this out from her doctor or so. Another important part, of course, is how much this will cost and how much her insurance (or any insurance for that matter, like provincial health insurance) will pay towards this. If it will cost too much to have her admitted, then she will have to stay with you or us. It will be impossible for her to travel to Holland. I hate to be so business like in this, but I also want you to find out what your mother's financial condition is: how much money has she left and what income does she receive or will she receive (e.g., from her present job, widow's pension, unemployment insurance, etc). It is also good to know if she has any debts or outstanding payments, say for hospital or drugs, flat, milkman, etc.

This reminds me, you should terminate her present lease, and don't forget that she may have paid a deposit with her first month's rent.

For your own sake, make sure that your mother has made a proper will and that all legal matters are settled. Check with your or her lawyer. Your mother has mentioned to Jane that she had made a will, but you can't be sure with her, now that her mind is so upset.

You have probably already inquired about all these points, but the more you can find out, especially regarding costs and insurance, the better we can make a decision when you get here.

Harry

Harry asks me to write something, too. There is very little to add to this letter. I doubt it, that she will be able to walk at all, when it is time to go to Toronto. I expect her to be bedridden every day from now on. It is very hard for you, to see her when you come to see us, so be prepared to see her much worse.

It seems very hard to go right away into financial inquiring, but I know from experience from friends, how expensive nursing homes are. They often do not, or hardly fall under insurance. It is, therefore, as Harry already writes, best to know most of these things. Of course, every province has its own regulations.

I find it especially mentally very hard to look after her, since it is so difficult to see somebody getting worse every day and knowing nothing can be done about it. All week she has been very confused, but today she seems much more alert. In a way, I like it better when she is confused; she is not so much aware of things and seems to be contented.

Let us know when you are coming and then we can talk things over.

Jane

Janneke (Jane) recounted a story to me of how she was concerned that she had given Bé too much pain medication one day. On October 2, 1966, Bé was having a good day. She asked Janneke to have lunch with her. They had tomato sandwiches, and Janneke sat by Bé's bed. At one point during lunch, Bé stood up, walked over to the glass door of her room and started waving. Janneke asked, "Tante Bé, who are you waiving to?" The reply: "Mama, Papa and Jaap." This reply made Janneke think she had given too much pain medication, causing Bé to hallucinate.

October 3, 1966, Andrea Pietrenella Johanna Bebelaar–Oltmans passes away. She was 54 years of age. Cause of death: carcinoma, breast, metastases, with contributing factors of pericarditis, acute pulmonary edema.

Walter doesn't make it to Montreal in time to say goodbye to his mother.

Letters of condolences start coming to Walter:

Eindhoven, October 6, 1966

Dear Wouter,

We received your telegram and it is very sad that you have no mother anymore. You also lost your dad when you were so young. For your mother, it was better this way, since there was nothing the doctors could do for her anymore.

When Opa and Oma died within 6 weeks, I was also totally devasted, although I had my parents for much longer than you had yours. It is a terrible shock not to have your parents anymore.

It will take time to get over this loss. But you still have your family, Wouter. You have Aunt Nel, myself and the Bebelaar family.

It is a difficult time now for you, Wouter, you have a lot to do now. All will be okay in the end. Stay strong; you are very courageous. Best regards for you, Shirley and a kiss for David.

Tante Kor.

A touching letter is received from a roommate of Bé's while she was in St. Michaels Hospital:

Thanksgiving Sunday
St. Michaels Hospital

Hello Mr. and Mrs. Bebelaar

I am sure you can picture just where I am sitting, trying to put on paper, my thoughts of these past few days.

I hope sincerely that you will still feel the benefit of your happy vacation, and by all means go to the same place next year, come that time again. It was your mother's wish. Each morning when our trays would come we'd casually be looking out of the window to see what kind of day it was and your wee mom would say, "Shirley and Walter are having another nice day today." Each day she would say, "It's the first real holiday they've had for 5 years. So, go next year. That's the way she'd want it.

Angie, as Pearl and I seemed to find it convenient to call her (and she told me one day that she liked it) suffered silently, then some days and nights she'd talk to me about it. I do feel in my heart that Angie would have had a hard time if she had gone back to her work. She'd say, "Catherine, how can I ever go back to do that work to sit?" I'd say, "With your personality, Angie, you can be the receptionist."

She loved wee David dearly, of course, and I used to refer back to the day (just before your vacation), him, looking at each of us, and telling us to take care of ourselves.

I do not know how much longer I'll be here, as I have never heard from Hillcrest Nursing home. I'd like just to go home to my own apartment and get to work slowly. Have had weekly visits with some (three) of the Reverend Gentlemen from Kew Beach Church, so I'll be thinking of you both when I arrive back and see the Auditorium, and when I get that far I can think of wee David. I'll bet he's awfully glad you both met, too.

Now I'm going to say So Long, just for now, but I do sincerely wish I could have been with you both for the 11 o'clock salute, on October 6 to the lady who you feel the much richer for making her acquaintance. I will always remember our days and nights together at St. Michael's. I remain, Your Friend Catherine.

Tante Kor sends Walter a second letter after Bé's passing.

Eindhoven, 14 October 1966

Dear Wouter,

How are you? It is not easy to lose your mother. It will take a lot of time to find yourself after such a loss. Eventuallly, you will find peace again.

I just received a 6-page letter from Janneke, in which she wrote a very informative account of how your mother's illness was. She went through a lot, your dear mother. But I can read how well Janneke and Harry have taken care of her. I think that with the pain she endured, and with her sometimes being a bit mixed up, that she was still happy in her last days. And knowing this, it is a consolation in the end. Why I write you this letter is the following: your mother had an old chest of drawers. That chest of drawers belonged to Opa's mother, and when she died he inherited that. Because I was named after my grandmother, I was promised this chest of drawers. When Opa and Oma died, then this chest of drawers was going to be your mother's. But should she return to Canada, the chest would go back to me.

This did not happen for some reason and that is not a problem. Now, I want to ask you to return this chest of drawers to Janneke. Janneke is named after Opa, and so I think this is a nice idea.

Janneke is not at all aware that I am asking this and I also don't know whether you would like to do this, but I would be very happy if you did. To send it back to me is not possible. And that is why I am asking you to give this to Janneke. I do not know your financial situation, but I think your mother had paid to refurbish this chest. You could ask Janneke to pay you back for that. But if you want to sell this chest, why not sell this to Janneke. This might sound a bit uneasy, so shortly after your mother's passing, but we live so far from each other, we cannot even speak about this together.

I hope you are going to do this. I would be very pleased if you did.

Is everything okay with you all, and how is David doing?

My best wishes for you three,

Tante Kor.

Walter receives a letter from Mrs. Angas. The Angas's are the family Bé and Walter worked for when they first came to Canada in 1955.

Mrs. Henry S. Angas
"Hindley"
Shanty Bay, Ontario

October 14th, 1966

My dear Walter,

The news of your mothers' death came as a great shock to us. One always hopes that all will be well, even in so serious an illness as overcame your mother.

She was a very courageous woman, but had a sad and difficult life, and I expect that all that brought her through that difficult period during the war, as a civilian prisoner of war was the need to protect and preserve you.

When I spoke to her just before she left for Montreal, she sounded so happy, and one can only be glad that she had this brief change before the end. It is certainly better that a hopeless illness should not be prolonged, and I do trust that she was not called so to suffer too much.

You had a mother whose memory you will be proud to know. I feel it was a privilege to have known her and had her with us for a time. It was a pleasure to see you and Shirley and your sweet son.

Mr. Angas and I leave soon for the winter, as we cannot cope with the snow and cold here without help. However, we sure hope to see you and the family again next summer.

With deepest sympathy and kindest regards.

Sincerely yours,

Edith B. Angas

Tante Nel writes to Walter about the passing of his mother, her sister.

Goedereede Oct. 1966

Dear Wouter and Shirley,

We received the sad news that your mother passed away. We are very sad. Your mother was not so old yet and to miss her at such an early age. A comforting thought is that she did not suffer long. We think of you all.

In her last letter she hoped to come to Holland once more, but from others we heard that was not possible anymore. Can you write us about her last days? Was she staying with Janneke?

How is it with you, Shirley and your little son? Maybe you can start saving money to visit your relatives in Holland. I telephone once in a while with Oma Bebelaar in Rotterdam. She is always so nice. Iek and Nely will move away from Goedereede to Oosterbeek. They have a nice house there. They had to wait 2 years before a house came available. It is beautiful around Oosterbeek. And it is not far, 2 hours driving.

Dear Wouter, we have to stay in contact. Write often. Cordial greetings, also from uncle Bram and cousin Jan and you, all three, love and kisses. Aunt Nel.

The daughter of a friend from The Dutch East Indies writes to Walter.

Bussum, 22 October 1966

Dear Wouter:

This week we received the horrible news that your mother passed away. We were all shocked and hope that you and your wife and the little boy will be strong to cope with this loss. We all knew that your mother had a serious operation a few years ago for cancer. We hoped that it was detected in time, that an operation could stop it. In her letters, she wrote about the check-ups done by her doctor, and she sounded optimistic. My father wrote her a letter a few months ago that she did not answer. I also wrote her recently for her birthday and worried that she was ill. Then last week, Oct. 17, my father telephoned me that he had received your letter with the sad news. My dad was very sad. He knew your mom for many years and my mother and your mother were special friends. They *shared so many experiences. First in the Dutch Indies and later, here, in Holland. We also laughed a lot with your mom and we shall not forget that. Also, she had a special place in my heart because she has helped Uncle Otto and myself.-For instance, in the-first years of our marriage we did not have a place to stay; your mom took us into her house. Maybe you remember it, when you lived in the Kerk Straat. You will miss her. She was the only one you had, and also you were the only one for her. And she will not see her grandson grow up. She was so proud of him. Because he looked so much like his dad. Wouter, I hope to hear from you occasionally and we keep contact. Would you have a photo of your mom for us? Cordial greetings for you and your wife and we wish you strength. Aunt Anneke*

December brings a letter from Rotterdam. The Bebelaar family send their condolences:

Rotterdam, 18 December 1966.

Dear Wouter, Shirley and Dave,

Finally, I find time to write you a letter. You must have thought I had forgotten about you, but that is far from the truth. I am always very busy. Grandmother was admitted in hospital to regulate her diabetes, and so I was the one to visit her. You know it is much better to live there because I went there every day and after 4 weeks she was discharged. But she has changed. It is quite a job now. Everything needs to be put on the scales and she now needs injections for her insulin. And the house is big, and so there is a lot to do. Three weeks ago she had a stroke, and the result of that is that walking is not so easy for her anymore and her speech is also affected. As you know, a big job. And every day people who visit her. I am so tired. Early out of bed and late in bed at night and to know that I am not a 20-year-old anymore, but that is how things are now.

You must have read in the letters from Aunt Yo that we have called many times talking about your mother, to find a way to fly her to Holland. But I heard on the phone from your Aunt in Zeeland that your mother was very ill. It was so difficult to talk about this and so a friend of her wrote her about this. She had sent some money to buy her something. Did you receive that? You should write her about this. She will be worried not to know, and she might ask the post office about this. We could not understand why her sisters never went over.

When I received your telegram – 7 in the morning – I have called Goeree and they would connect me and I have called Aunt Yo and Frans and Nico and they too have informed the other family.

I was so happy to receive a letter from Gerrit, that he had been to visit you. Your aunt called me to also give some money to send flowers. But later she called me that they had not done this because it was too late. I thought that it was such a shame since you might have thought that we had forgotten about you. On the contrary! We talk a lot about your mother. I am so glad that Opa did not have to go through this all, it would have been devastating for him.

How is your son, Wouter? Gerrit said that he is a true Bebelaar. I hope your wife is feeling better now. You should write us because I do not hear much from you. The other family members are all well.

I have to end this letter, dear Wouter, I need to start doing things here.

Best regards from all of us and also from Grandmother and happy holidays and lots of love for you all,

Your Mams

1967

During the summer of 1967, Walter returns to Montreal with his family. They stay with Janneke and Harry. As a child, I didn't understand the signifigance of this trip. In retrospect, this was a family trip to EXPO 76, but more importantly, it was an opportunity for Walter to exercise the demons of not having been with his mother at her passing.

1970

August of 1970 brings a second son for Walter. He chooses to honour Geritt, an uncle on the Bebelaar side of the family, naming his son after him by the English version of the name, Gary.

1973

In June of 1973, Walter takes his family on a trip to Holland. This is the first time he has returned to Holland since 1955. He is now 33 years of age, with a wife and two sons. The trip encompasses visits with all available family members from the Bebelaar and Oltmans families. Visits are made to the homes of Walter's aunts, Kor and Nel, where he is able to rekindle memories of his childhood. All the uncles from the Bebelaar family are visited as is the one aunt from the Bebelaar family who has just delivered her first child.

Over the next 36 years, Walter has the opportunity to travel to the Netherlands several times, associated with his work in International Shipping and personal visits to stay connected with family. His final visit in 2008 includes an emotional trip to Bronbeek Museum in Arnhem, where he sees his father's name on a wall, honouring KNIL soldiers who died in defence of the Dutch territory of Indonesia. This is an especially emotional trip for Walter, as he knows that it is his last. Seven years earlier, he was diagnosed with cancer, and he is becoming increasingly frail. This is his opportunity to say goodbye to the family he feels so connected to, despite the distance between Canada and the Netherlands.

July 5, 2009, at 2:00 a.m. Walter passes quietly in his sleep, with his two sons by his side. Cause of death is chronic lymphatic lymphoma.

A funeral for Walter is held, and includes family from the Netherlands, family friends, business colleagues and his golf friends. His mother is also honoured at the time of his burial. To his resting spot, is added the watch his mother had during the years she spent in the Japanese prisoner of war camps. This watch is sent with him to his final resting spot, as it had contributed to him staying alive.

During the years in the camps, food was scarce. In order to feed her son and herself, Bé bartered with the locals, through the fence, for food. During the barter, she would take the food through the fence, holding the watch out as payment. As the individual went to take the watch, young Wouter would reach through the fence, hitting them in the shins to distract them, so his mother could pull the watch back through the fence, giving them an opportunity for another meal in the future.

Since the passing of my father, I have had time to reflect on his story, and that of my grand-parents. As a father, I want to be able to provide information to my children about their family history. My dad had no recollection of his father, as he was less than two years old when the war started in the Pacific. I was three years old when my Oma passed away, leaving me with no memory of her. I needed to find out about the character of my Opa and Oma, so I could give my children a sense of where they came from. The first task was to take all the letters that I was left with when my father passed. A bin full of letters and memorabilia, that to this day, I do not understand how some of these items survived the war.

As the process of translating the documents occurred, I discovered things about my Opa that no one in the family knew about, and things about my Oma that had never been discussed. I needed to honour them. This was written to do just that.

What Was Discovered

SS *Van Imhoff*

Following the German invasion of the Netherlands in 1940, all Germans in the Dutch East Indies were interned. Then:

> after the Japanese attack on Pearl Harbor prisoner transports were assembled on the west coast of Sumatra, which should bring the interned Germans from a Japanese invasion of British India. Two of these transports with Dutch ships actually arrived in Bombay. The third ship to be used for such transport was the freighter *Van Imhoff*. He left on 18 January 1942 in Sibolga.
>
> On January 19, 1942, a Japanese aircraft west of Sumatra attacked *Van Imhoff*, who was not labeled as a prisoner transport, assuming that it was a Dutch troop-carrier. On board were 478 German civilian internees and a crew of 110 Dutchmen. With the sinking of *Van Imhoff*, the entire Dutch team went with Captain Hoeksema in the lifeboats. German civilian internees, who were trapped on and below deck with barbed wire, were banned from going into the boats under threat of shooting. Most civilian internees sank by ship. Among the victims was the artist Walter Spies.
>
> Some people were able to save themselves on two remaining small boats without rudders and emergency rations and some rafts and were spotted the next day by a flying boat of the Dutch Navy. This called the Dutch steamer *Boelongan* to help,

who arrived at about 9.20 clock on the first lifeboat. When the captain of the *Boelongan*, ML Berveling, learned that the shipwrecked people were exclusively German civilian internees, he had them turned off without having to comply with the request for drinking water and food or accommodation on board, as he had received the following instructions:

> "First pick up the crew of the steamship Van Imhoff, the European and inland ship's crew as well as the soldiers who were on board for security – then on the instruction of the military commander take on board reliable elements among the German internees (who were transported with ss Van Imhoff) – prevent other Germans from landing."

A few minutes later, another lifeboat, two rafts and castaways were spotted in the water from the *Catalina*, which was supposed to protect the ship from underwater attacks. At 10.40, the *Boelongan*, which was being directed there, was on-site, but again took none of the shipwrecked onboard. Shortly after the *Boelongan* had passed the shipwrecked vehicles, an aircraft attack on the steamer was observed from the Y-63. Berveling's statements, claiming to have been attacked several times by the Japanese plane, did not coincide with testimony from survivors in the lifeboat and observations made by the crew of the Y-63, who claimed that the plane had turned off after dropping a single bomb. The inmates of the boats separated on January 21, 1942 from the castaways on the slow rafts, in the hope of being able to send this later help.

Only 65 people were able to be saved on January 23, 1942 on the island of Nias; all the rest were killed.

(Source: "Versenkung Der Van Imhoff." Wikipedia. August 10, 2018. Accessed August 17, 2018. https://de.wikipedia.org/wiki/Versenkung_der_Van_Imhoff.)

Dorusz Ras, in a letter to Bé Bebelaar-Oltmans after the war, mentioned he had never seen Jaap's fountain pen but thought he might have lost it on the *Van Imhoff*. Based on the timing, this indicates Jacob Bebelaar was one of the KNIL (Royal Netherlands East Indies Army) soldiers aboard the ship when it was sunk by the Japanese. This was the first that anyone in the family knew that Jaap had been on that ship.

Jaap's POW Card

The following images show a scanned copy of Jaap's POW (prisoner of war) Internment card.

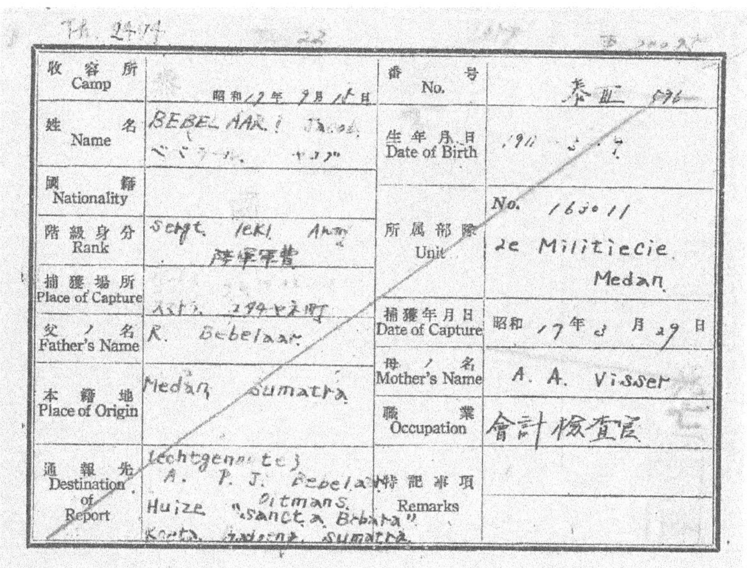

収容所 Camp	昭和17年9月15日	番号 No.	[illegible]
姓名 Name	BEBELAAR, Jacob	生年月日 Date of Birth	1911
國籍 Nationality		所属部隊 Unit	No. 163011 2e Militiecie Medan
階級身分 Rank	Sergt. KNIL Army 陸軍軍曹		
捕獲場所 Place of Capture	[illegible]	捕獲年月日 Date of Capture	昭和17年3月29日
父ノ名 Father's Name	R. Bebelaar	母ノ名 Mother's Name	A. A. Visser
本籍地 Place of Origin	Medan Sumatra	職業 Occupation	會計検査官
通報先 Destination of Report	Echtgenote: A. P. J. Bebelaar-Oltmans Huize "Sancta Barbara" Kota Radja, Sumatra	特記事項 Remarks	

補修欄 Other Informations

昭和18年6月22日 赤痢ニテ死亡ス 土葬

昭和18 22日死亡 (JA. 95 1358)

22 June 1943 Died of Dysentery (Interment)

(Source: Received from www.s-o-o.nlinfo@s-o-.nl, as found on website Stichting Oorlogsgetroffenen in De Oost - Contact. Accessed December 16, 2014 http://pow.s-o-o.nl/Contact/)

Jacob Bebelaar's POW Internment Card translated into English

Transfer Date 1	15/09/1942
Camp Number	596
Name	Bebelaar, Jacob
Date of Birth	09/05/1911
Nationality	Netherlands
Rank	Sergeant 1st Class, Army
Unit	2nd Militia Company, Medan
Studbook number	163011
Place of Capture	Kutacane, Sumatra
Date of Capture	29/03/1942
Occupation	Auditor

Father's Name	R. Bebelaar
Mother's Name	A.A. Visser (deceased)
Place of Origin	Medan, Sumatra
Destination of Report	husband of A. P. J. Bebelaar-Oltmans, "Santa Barbara" house, Kota Gadang, Sumatra
Remarks	82044

Camp Area Jurisdiction:

Transfer date 1: Thai POW Camp 05/09/1942

Camp name and registration no.	
1st camp	No.3 Branch Camp of Thai, POW Camp 596
2nd camp	Main Camp of Thai POW Camp 20095

Other Information (Backside of the card)
Fell ill on 1 June 1943
Died of bacillary dysentery on 22 June 1943 at 20:30
22 June 1943 (Burial)
Died on 22 June 1943 (JA.5 P.1359)
Place of Death: Payathonzu Detached Camp of No.3 Branch Camp of Thai POW Camp
Disposal of remains: Buried at Payathonzu Cemetery of the camp (JA180)

The following information was received from info@s-o-o.nl on March 17, 2015. No.3 Branch Camp of Thai POW Camp was officially set up in Thambyuzayat in Burma on 16 August 1942. The Japanese camp commander was Lt. Col. Yoshitada Nagatomo. No. 3 Branch Camp was in charge of the Thai/Burma border area construction, such as Songkurai (294km), Chaunggahlaya (303km), Payarhonzu, Three Pagoda path (108/307km), Angganung(105/310km), Regue (100/315km), Kyondaw (95/319km). There were 9,368 POWs in total in the camp. The POWs were divided into two groups. The 3,302 POWs were moved to Angganung detached camp, which was 108 km from

Thanbyuzayat. The 6,066 POWs were sent to Payathonzu detached camp, which was 105 km from Thanbyuzayat. Before the construction ended, the No.3 Branch camp moved to Mezali in September 1943. After the completion of the Birma-Siam Railway, the camp moved to Angganung for maintenance and again moved to Thamakan in April 1944. The camp discontinued in August 1944. No.3 Branch Camp of Thai POW Camp was asked to work for No.5 Railway Regiment, but because of the shortage of manpower, part of Angganung and Payathonzu detached camps were placed under the command of No.9 Railway Regiment.

(JA.5 P.1359) is "death certificated" created by Japanese camp authority and Dutch military doctor. The record is held at Ministry of Welfare, Tokyo Japan. The inventory is JA.5, his record might be written on page 1359. Please contact us if you wish to obtain the record.

For further information, please look at the following websites:

- *Gebruik* of the database (by Kaori Maekawa and POW Research Network Japan at Nationaal Archief, den Haag) http://www.gahetna.nl/collectie/ index/ nt00425 /gebruik
- *Stamp list* in the database (by Kaori Maekawa at Nationaal Archief, den Haag) http://www.gahetna.nl/sites/default/files/bijlagen/stamp list logo.pdf
- POW camps in Japan (POW Research Network Japan) http://www.powresearch.jp/en/ archive/ camp list/ index.html#shuuyoujo
- POW camps outside Japan (POW Research Network Japan) http://www.powresearch.jp/en/ archive/ camp list/ outside index.html

(Source: Received from www.s-o-o.nlinfo@s-o-.nl, as found on website Stichting Oorlogsgetroffenen in De Oost - Contact. Accessed March 17, 2015 http://pow.s-o-o.nl/Contact/)

Jaap's POW Journey

From the POW card, we know that on March 29, 1942, Jaap was captured by the Japanese in Kutacane, Sumatra. He was then sent to Medan, arriving March 31, where he was held as a POW. On May 5, 1942 he was part of a group that was loaded onto the SS *Kyokusei Maru* and sent to Tavoy, Burma.

Kampong Union, Belawan, N. Sumatra

Belawan was de havenstad van Medan (aan de Oost-kust van Sumatra).Belawan was the port city of Medan (on the eastern coast of Sumatra). Het kamp Unie Kampong was een gebouwencomplex in het havengebied.The camp, Kampong Union, was a building complex in the port area.Het kamp bestond uit een gedeelte voor krijgsgevangenen en een gedeelte voor burger-geïnterneerden (het "burgerkamp"), van elkaar gescheiden door prikkeldraad. The camp consisted of two sections separated by barbed wire: one for prisoners of war and one for civilian internees (the "citizen camp").

Camp commander: Lieutenant Oda

Camp Guard: Japanese military

Camp Leadership: Major C.F. Hazenberg

Transports:

date	gotten from	left to	number of per transport	number of in camp	type persons
31-03-1942	Aceh		2500	2500	kr
31-03-1942	Padang		600	3100	kr (1)
11-05-1942	Bir: Prison		100	3200	kr

15-05-1942		Bur: Mergui (2)	500		kr (3)
15-05-1942		Bur: Tavoy (4)	1200	1500	kr (5)
01-06-1942		Environment (6)	20		kr (7)
02-06-1942	Koeta Raja		300	1800	kr (8)
xx-06-1942		Released	300	1500	kr (9)
17-06-1942	Padang (10)		500	2000	kr (11)
20-06-1942		Lawesigalagala	?		kr (12)
xx-06-1942	Lawesigalagala		5		kr
26-06-1942		Med: Gloegoer	1200	0	kr (13)

kr = prisoner of war
Bir = Biruën, Bur = Burma, Med = Medan

(1) British prisoner of war
(2) with the *England Maru 1*
(3) all Englishmen
(4) **with the *Kyokusei Maru***
(5) **all led by Dutch Major Hazenberg**
(6) to various hospitals
(7) Doctors
(8) indigenous soldiers
(9) about the group of native soldiers, who were interned here on 02-06-1942
(10) and Fort de Kock (via Kabandjahe)
(11) Dutch and British prisoner of war
(12) 110 prisoner of war of Indo-European origin and an unknown number of indigenous soldiers
(13) Dutch, English and Australian prisoner of war

Proceedings: loading and unloading of ships and railcars, including ammunition

SS *Kyokusei Maru*

COUNTRY	CITY	1st CAMP	A/V	DATE	kr	KILL
Sumatra	Belawan		V	16-5-1942	1200	
Birma	Victoria Point		A	20-5-1942	1200	
	Mergui		A	24-5-1942	1200	
	Tavoy		A	26-5-1942	1200	
		Tavoy	A	26-5-1942	1200	

A = Arrival, V = Departure; kr = prisoner of war
(1) Dutch

The *Kyokusei Maru* (5493 tons in 1920, sometimes referred to as *Chiloup*) departed on 16-5-1942 from Belawan with 1,200 Dutch prisoners of war, together with the *England Maru 1* with 500 British prisoners of war. All these prisoners of war who had recently been in Belawan, arrived from Padang. In the Strait of Malacca locks, these two ships joined a convoy of several ships, which a day earlier departed from Singapore, including the Celebes *Maru 1*, the *Toyohashi Maru* and any escort ships.

On 20-5-1942 reached the convoy, Victoria Point; here a part of the prisoner of war was aboard the *Toyohashi Maru* deposed.

On 24-5-1942 reached the convoy, Mergui; here the prisoner of war of the *Celebes Maru 1* and that of the *England Maru 1* were deposited.

On 26-5-1942 reached (the rest of) the convoy Tavoy, including *Kyokusei Maru* with the 1200 Dutch prisoner of war; they were brought ashore here.

Note: From some diary of Dutch prisoner of war shows that both ships, which departed from Belawan, were Dutch. Possibly there was therefore a (small) part of the Dutch in the *England Maru 1*.

Tavoy, Burma

Tavoy is on the west coast of southern Burma, approximately the height of Bangkok.

After debarking, the men were housed in a rice mill on the quay. The next day they went to Tavoy. The camp consisted of an abandoned mission (Methodist School): a big, solid two-storey building, a boarding school, some houses and some classrooms. There was also a jungle camp and an airport camp.

Camp Leadership: Major Hazenberg

Transports:

date	gotten from	left to	number per transport	number in camp	type people
26-05-42 (1)	Singapore (2)		1000	1000	kr (3)
30-05-42 (1)	Belawan (4)		1200	2200	kr (5)
06-06-1942		Ye			kr
05-08-1942		Ye			kr
10-08-1942	Mergi		1500		kr (6)
10-08-1942	Victoria Point		1000		kr (7)
16-09-42 (8)		Thanb – 415 (9)		0	kr

kr = prisoner of war; Thanb = Thanbyuzayat

(1) as of this date splitting into different groups on consecutive days
(2) with *Toyohashi Maru*, leaving Singapore 14-5-1942
(3) (Australians
(4) *England Maru* 1, leaving Belawan 15-5-1942 (on arrival from port to camp 33 km walk)
(5) Dutch
(6) 1000 500 Australians and Englishmen
(7) Australians

(8) as of this date in various transports
(9) by ship to Moulmein, followed by trucks (total 2 days)

Activities:

- chores in the city (including loading-and-unloading), airport construction (in the city), repair of a bridge (in the jungle)

Conditions:

- nutrition: mostly bad
- live: sufficient space
- water: running water (the Younger: water from one well)
- health: on arrival: bacillary dysentery (by road drinking water from contaminated pond)
- spiritual care: Mak pastor, Father Vergeest
- deaths: by dysentery; 8 Australians escaped 30-05-1942, caught, executed

Ye, Burma

Ye lay on the west coast, about 30 miles south of Thanbyuzayat. Here the railway from Moulmein ended south through Thanbyuzayat.

The camp - the so-called city-camp - was housed in kampong houses. There was also a jungle camp, where groups of prisoner of war had to build a road. The camp was first a labor camp, later a transit camp.

Camp commander: "Beech Mans" (hit hard and often with his fists)

Camp Leadership: Ome Keesje (KNIL Major)

Transports:

date	gotten from	left to	number of per transport	number of in camp	type persons
06-06-1942	Tavoy (1)		1000		kr (2)
08-06-1942	Mergi		200		kr (3)
05-08-1942	Tavoy				kr
06-08-42 (4)		Thanbyu - 415 (5)		0 0	kr

kr = prisoner of war; Thanbyu = Thanbyuzayat

(1) by truck to river with boat crossing, continue by train
(2) Mainly Dutch
(3) Australians
(4) from this date in various transports
(5) walking along the railway, part of the luggage trolleys

Activities (urban camp):

- June-August 1942:??

Activities (jungle camp):

- construction road somewhere in the jungle (several hundred workers), little supervision, little discipline

Conditions (urban camp):

- nutrition: reasonable, sometimes a cow available, shopping in the city; to cook (wet wood)
- live: 40 to 50 men after 70 to 80 people per house
- bless you: sick in two small barracks; 17 Dutch severe tropical ulcers
- deaths: some men escaped, caught, executed
- climate: very heavy rain

Moulmein Prison, Burma

Moulmein was on the west coast of the country, about 60 km north of Thanbyuzayat, the beginning of the Burma railway.

Transports:

date	gotten from	lef to	number of per trans-port	number of in camp	type of persons
GROUP 1	SUMATRA-FORCE				
xx-06-1942	Singapore (1)		1500	1500	kr (2)
xx-xx-1942		Thanbyu - 415	1500	0	kr
GROUP 2					
16-09-42 (3)	Tavoy (4)		4000	4000	kr
17-09-42 (3)		Thanbyu - 415			kr
GROUP 3	*Maebashi Maru 1*				
25-10-1942	Rank: prison (5)		1800	1800	kr
xx-10-1942		Thanbyu - 415	1800	0	kr
GROUP 4	*Tacoma Maru 1*				
22-12-1942	Rank: prison (6)		600	600	kr (7)
24-12-1942		Thanbyu - 415 (8)	200	400	kr
26-12-1942		Thanbyu - 415 (8)	200	200	kr
30-12-1942		Thanbyu - 415 (8)	200	0	kr
26-01-1943	Rank: Prison		700		kr (9)
xx-xx-1943		Thanbyu - 415 (8)		0	kr
GROUP 5	*NN NN Maru Maru 3 and 18*				
28-12-1942	Rank: Prison		1000	1000	kr
29-12-1942		Thanbyu - 415	1000	0	kr
xx-01-1943	Rank: Prison		400	400	kr
xx-01-1943		Thambyu - 415	400	0	kr
GROUP 6	*Nichimei Maru Maru Moji 2*				
17-01-1943	Singapore (10)		3000	3000	kr
xx-01-1943		Thanbyu - 415 (11)			kr
xx-01-1943		Camp 18		0	kr

kr = prisoner of war

Grade = Rangoon Thanbyu = Thanbyuzayat, prison = Prison

(1) with *Celebes Maru 2*, leaving Singapore 15-06-1942
(2) Williams Force, mostly Australians led by Lt-Col Williams
(3) **in several shipments from that date; always one night in Moulmein**
(4) **largely by ship; partly overland via Ye**
(5) *Yamagata Maru 1* (from Singapore arrived with *Maebashi Maru 1*)
(6) with *Yamagata Maru 2*, in a night and a morning
(7) group 4A, with the *Tacoma Maru 1* came from Singapore to Rangoon
(8) to train boxcars, about 2 hours
(9) group 4B, with the *Tacoma Maru 1* came from Singapore to Rangoon
(10) *Nichimei Maru* and *Moji Maru 2*, leaving Singapore 10-01-1943
(11) according Bomb: on 28-01-1943 directly from Moulmein to Hlapauk - 397 (18)

Conditions (Group IV):

- state: no war in the city seen

Conditions (Group IV):

- live: sleeping on the floor, sick on iron beds without mattresses
- medical care: Kees Camp nurse; from Thanbyuzayat: doctor Bloemsma

Thanbyuzayat Line - 415 (0) Burma

Thailand 3B (since 16-8-1942)

Thanbyuzayat lay on the existing railway from Ye to Moulmein (both on the coast). Here the construction of the Burma Railway began in the direction of Thailand.

The camp (an old cooling camp) was a labor camp (loading of construction material) and a hospital camp (care of the sick from the camps along the Burma Railway). It was the headquarters of department/group denoted III (total about 10,000 prisoner of war spread over 100 km railway: 200 groups of 50 male).

Camp Commanders: Colonel Nagatomo (head of department / group III)
Camp Guard: Koreans (including "The Shouter")
Camp Leadership: Brigadier A.L. Varley (for entire department/group 3)
Interpreter: Cornel Lumiere
Transports:

date	gotten from	left to	number of per transport	number of in camp	type of persons
	Camp: incoming				
xx-06-1942	Moul: Prison (1)		1500	1500	kr (2)
xx-08-1942	Moul: Prison (3)		4700	6200	kr (4)
xx-10-1942	Moul: Prison (5)		1800	8000	kr (6)
xx-11-1942	Moul: Prison (7)		1800	10,000	kr (8)
xx-12-1942	Moul: Prison (9)		1000	11,000	kr (10)
xx-01-1943	Moul: Prison (11)		2000 (a)	13,000	kr (12)
	Camp: outgoing				
24-09-1942		Wegali - 407 (8)	1400		kr
25-10-1942		Hlapauk - 397 (18)			kr
22-06-43 (B)				0	kr
	SICK CAMP				
22-06-1943		Wegali - 407 (8)			zkr
22-06-1943		Hlapauk - 397 (18)			zkr
22-06-1943		Aparon - 332 (83)			zkr
22-06-1943		Anga-2-315 (100)		0	zkr

kr = prisoner of war, zkr = sick prisoner of war
Anga-2 = Anganum-2, Moul = Moulmein

(1) Group 2, finishing with *Celebes Maru 2*
(2) 1500 Australians (A force led by Brigadier ALVarley)
(3) **Group 1 arriving via Tavoy 4 ships**
(4) **3,000 Australians, 500 British, Dutch 1200**
(5) Group 3 arrival *Maebashi Maru 1*
(6) 1 500 Australians, 200 Americans, 100 Dutch
(7) Group 4, arriving with *Tacoma Maru Maru 1* and *Shinyu*
(8) 1400 Dutch *(Tacoama Maru 1)*, 400 others
(9) Group 5, with arrival *NN NN Maru Maru 3* and *18*
(10) 1000 Dutch (part of Java Party 5B)
(11) Group 6, arriving with *Moji Maru 2*
(12) 1000 Dutch on *Nichimei Maru*, and 1000 others
(A) a part of this group went straight from Moulmein to Camp 8
(B) the camp was evacuated in connection with sustained bombing

<u>Administration:</u>

Here are the lists of names of the prisoner of war were made under Captain Griffin, 6-fold, the Japanese Hayashi demanded flawless lists, improvements were not allowed (see Lumiere pg 92)

<u>Proceedings:</u>

- From August 1942: building material and tool loading and unloading; make railway sleepers
- August-September 1942: railway construction to Wegali

<u>Circumstances:</u>

- nutrition: well, grocery purchase additional
- live: large number of standard barracks
- bless you: sick in separate hospital-hut
- medical care: Bloemsma doctor; nurse Corbeau
- spiritual care: Reverend Mak

Wegali Line - 407 (8) Burma

Wegale, Wagalé, Camp 8

This camp was located 407 km from Non Pladuk and 8 km from Thanbyuzayat; it was the first camp on the Burma Railway, calculated from Thanbyuzayat. Later it was (after the bombing Thanbyuzayat) temporary hospital camp.

Camp Guard: Koreans

Camp Leadership: Major Hazenberg; Major J.H. de Vries; Detiger

Transports:

date	gotten from	left to	number of per transport	number of in camp	type of persons
	Camp				
24-09-1942	Thanb - 415 (0)		1400	1400	kr (1)
xx-11-1942	??		100	1500	kr (2)
23-02-1943		Anak – 369 (46) (3)	1300	200	kr
27-02-1943		Retpu – 385 (30)	200	0	kr
	SICK CAMP				
22-06-1943	Thanb - 415 (0)				zkr
01-07-1943		Retpu – 385 (30)			zkr

kr = prisoner of war, zkr = sick prisoner of war
Anak = Anakwin, Thanb = Thanbyuzayat

(1) **Dutch, part of the A-Force (group from Belawan)**
(2) from Java
(3) on trucks

Proceedings:

- September 1942 - February 1943: construction embankment between 5 and 12 km marker, daily 1,000 men (including officers); groups of 50 male; task: 1, later 2, even 3 m per person per day; long working hours (6-19 hours)

Conditions (labor):

- nutrition: bad, too few vegetables, no beans
- live: sleep on branches, open barracks
- bathe: in potash behind the camp
- plumbing: bad
- bless you: poor, many sick
- climate: in winter, cold nights
- escape: 4 men escaped, one road deceased, three caught and slain in Thanbyuzayat

Retpu Line - 385 (30) Burma

Retpou, Retpau, Redpoo, Camp 30

This camp was located at 385 km from Non Pladuk and 30 km from Thanbyuzayat. This camp was first a great camp, later (from April 1943) a little sick camp.

Camp Commanders: Lieutenant Naito

Transports:

date	gotten from	left to	number of per trans-port	number of in camp	type of persons
	Camp				
26-12-1942	Thanb. - 415 (0) (1)				kr (2)
xx-03-1943		Payath - 307 (108)			kr
13-03-1943		Mezali - 345 (70)			kr
15-05-1943	Hlapauk – 397 (18)				kr (3)

	SICK CAMP				
01-07-1943	Wegali - 407 (8)			2000	zkr
04-10-43 (4)		Payath - 307 (108) (5)		0	zkr

kr = prisoner of war, zkr = sick prisoner of war
Payath = Payathonzu, Thanb = Thanbyuzayat

(1) by truck
(2) group of the *Tacoma Maru* Java Party 5
(3) British battalion (Sumatra Party)
(4) and next days
(5) according to Walker, pg 591 (also) to "camp Kohn Kahn = 55"

Proceedings:

- January - March 1943: railway embankment construction process Retpu-Anakwin (15 km), work had to be completed in 2 months
- May 1943: loading and unloading train / car (even at night)

Circumstances:

- nutrition: very bad
- live: in barracks
- bathe: in near river
- bless you: many dysentery, very much sick, seriously ill to **Thanbyuzayat** (camp hospital)
- deaths: 1 to 2 per day

Payathonzu Line - 307 (108) Burma:

Pajatonzu, Camp 108

This camp was located 307 km and 108 km of Non Pladuk Thanbyuzayat. It was about the Three Pagodas Pass, 500 meters from the border between Burma and Thailand on Burmese territory.

Camp Commanders: Lieutenant Osoda (Osada)

Camp Guard: Koreans (including “The Howler”)

Camp Leadership: Superior Platte; Detiger; de Vries

Transports:

date	gotten from	left to	number of per trans-port	number of in camp	type of persons
xx-03-1943	Retpu - 385 (30)				kr (1)
12-05-1943	Mezali - 345 (70)		1000		kr
xx-09-1943		Niki-Niki - 282	200		kr
xx-xx-1943		Anganum - 310 (105)	400		kr
04-10-1943	Rabao - 397 (18)				kr
31-10-1943	Retpu - 385 (30)				
14-11-1943				2600	kr (2)
10-01-1944 10-(3)		Khangar - 301 (114) (4)			kr
xx-02-1944		Tamarkan - 55			zkr

kr = prisoner of war
Khangar = Changarraya

(1) almost all Dutch, part of the A-Force;
(2) according to Wim Kan, pg 190;
(3) in groups of 200 to man 31-01-1944
(4) may also directly to Sunkurai - 294 (121) and Niki-Niki - 282 (133)

Proceedings:

- May-September 1943: railway embankment construction
- From September 1943: railway maintenance, construction roadway beside the railway, chopping wood for locomotives

<u>Circumstances:</u>

- nutrition: very poor, very hungry; canteen almost always empty
- live: dark barracks, bald camp; in the rainy season mud everywhere, all dirty
- water: inadequate
- hygiene: many pests, including lice, rats
- medical care: surgeon Cotes (Australian), nurse Wood Splitters
- bless you: very poor, many deaths ("camp of death"); seriously ill to Tamarkan-55
- state: horrible

This was the end of the journey for Jaap. He passed away June 22, 1943 at Camp 108.

Bé and Wouter's POW Journey

When the Japanese conquered Sumatra in March 1942, women and children were sent to internment camps. From the two message cards that Jaap sent, we know that Bé and Wouter went to Brastagi. The camp at Brastagi was the location of the Planters' Association boarding school.

Brastagi, N. Sumatra

Brastagi is 60 km south of Medan on the way to Kaban Djahe and Lake Toba. The camp was housed in various buildings of the Charleston School, a boarding school for the Planters' Association.

Camp Commanders: Captain Kibitaicho others

Camp Guard: Molasses or Mulassai ("Uncle Molly", by 6:43), Hosoda, Inga Rashi ("Tiger")

Camp Leadership: Hr J. M. Marsman (16:04:42 - 04/29/42), Mr. J. van Eck (01:05:42 to 01:06:42), Mr. J.C. Cook (per 01:06:42); Mr. A. H. Tournai (per 10:08:42), Ms. Nora Prince and Ms. Ria Eikens

Transports (according to Atlas Japanese Kampen):

date	gotten from	left to	number of per trans-port	number of in camp	type of persons
16:04:42	Surroundings		939		Mon, Fri, ki
28/04/42		Kabandjahe: HIS	6		mom
05/26/42	Kab: Zend. Hospital		20 (1)		Mon, Fri
10:10:42	Bra: St Luïdina-kl (2)		94		Fri, ki
21:12:42	PS: SDF		697		Fri, ki
21:12:42				**1744**	**Mon, Fri, ki**
27.04.43 (2)		Med Poelau Bra ABCE	200		Fri, ki
31/05/43		Med: Sungei Sengkol	34		jo
19:06:43		Med: Sungei Sengkol	8		mom
29/06/43	Kabandjahe		21		Mon, Fri, ki
5:08:43	Kab: leprosarium		14		Mon, Fri, ki
9:09:43		Med Poelau Bra ABCE	5		Fri, ki
14:10:43	Kab: Zend. Hospital		15		Mon, Fri, ki
17:02:44		Med: Sungei Sengkol	18		jo
17:02:44		Med: Belawan Estate	3		jo
xx.03.44		Med: Sungei Sengkol	?		jo
8:06:44	Lawesigalagala		13		Fri, ki
14.12.44 (4)		RP: Si Rengorengo	182 (5)		jo order
10:02:45		Med Gloegoer II	18		Fri, ki
6.13.45 (6)		RP: Aek Pamienke III	1347	0 (6)	Fri, ki

Abbreviations / Nuts

jo = boys, ki = children, ma = men, no = nuns to old = ma, ov = ancient Fri, vr = women, zi = sick

Bra = Brastagih Kab = Kabandjahe, Med = Medan, PS = Pematangsiantar, RP = Rantau Prapat
St Luïdina-kl = St Luïdina clinic, Poelau Bra = Poelau Brajan

(1) 12 men and 8 women
(2) acted as "maternity hospital": nuns helped births; then women went back to the camp
(3) and 04/28/43
(4) and 15:12:44
(5) 169 13 boys and old men
(6) A total of 26 deaths

As the Japanese were taking losses in the war, prisoners were moved to concentrate them in a few camps. June 13, 1945, they were moved to Aek Pamienke III. When the war ended on August 15, 1945, and the camps were disbanded, the following is the roster of prisoners in Aek Pamienke III.

Rantau Prapat, Aek Pamienke III, N. Sumatra

Roster Hong 1 (244 people)

(Source: Journals North Sumatra in wartime, 1945 AP III, pg 212-213)

NAME = name (initials are missing)
Column 2: number of children under 6 years (total 63)
Column 3: number of children over 6 years (total 82)
Column 4: Total number of persons per household (total 244)
NR = rank in the original list

NAME	<6 yr	> 6 yr	total	NR
Asperen, of	1		2	2
Baker-Vegtink, R.	2		3	78
Bebelaar	1		2	48
Mountains,	2		3	10
Better			1	16

Ax, van der		4	5	45
Blanksma-zur Keinsm.	2		3	3
Bloemendal at	2	1	4	29
Boer van Loo, the	1	1	3	25
Bordes, the	1		2	74
Brown Braun	1	3	5	52
Brown-Brouwer, the		1	2	75
Bruyn Bruins	1	2	3	70
Corver	1		2	40
Dijkhuis		2	3	46
Dolmans		3	4	49
Tournai	1	2	4	42
Dort, of	1	1	3	54
Driessen, of	1	1	3	39
Driessen-Stavast	1	1	3	73
Duinker		1	3	13
Ebbink		1	2	38
Elema		2	3	79
Eyseren, of	1		2	61
Geddie		2	3	26
Gisbertsz	1	1	3	28
Great	1	1	3	63
Groteboer		1	2	30
Haagmans	1		2	43
Hasenack	2	1	4	6
Corner	1		2	71
Karelse	2	2	5	14
Church Camp	1	2	4	60
Koerselman		3	4	66
King, the	1	1	3	56
Koole	1	3	5	32
Koolstra	2		3	47
Koops	1		2	15
Kuipers-Korsten	1	1	3	4
Laurens		2	3	9
Leeuwarden, of	1		2	69
Looyen		2	3	22

Meuse (Leader)		2	3	11
Marel, of the	1	2	3	17
Meulen, van der	1	1	3	1
Meyers	1	1	3	24
Mill Burgh	1		2	55
Monsma	2		3	53
Walnut tree			1	50
Overbeek	1	3	5	7
Overdijking			1	59
Paul	1		2	44
Plank, van der	1	3	5	31
Pol	1	2	4	18
Polak		2	3	64
Rhee, of	1		2	62
Ritsema van Eck	1		2	36
Saeys	1	1	3	37
Schuurmans	1		2	23
Simon			1	68
Signs			1	33
Teutscher	2		3	19
Owl	2	2	5	72
Vacqier			1	51
Vaes	1		2	77
Pig Fisherman	1	3	5	27
Veen, van der	1		2	76
Verschuren	1		2	35
Verwey		2	3	8
Voute		3	4	34
Waaker	1	1	3	5
Wardenburg-van der Vlugt		1	2	12
Weisfelt	1		2	57
Wezel, of		1	2	58
Wheels, van der		1	2	65
Wijngaart, the	1	2	4	67
Yosina Rompah			1	20
Sailor	1		2	41
Swan	2	2	5	21

When they left the camp, they boarded trains to go back to Medan. Ironically, the Japanese soldiers became their protectors, as the Indonesians wanted Independence from the Netherlands, and radical factions were attacking Dutch citizens as they left the camps.

Once back in Medan, arrangements were made for Bé and Wouter to board the *S.S. Noordam* on January 20, 1946, for the return voyage back to Holland.

The Final Honour

After investing time to learn about my Opa and Oma and learning about how they endured in circumstances that no one should have to endure, I knew there was more to be done. Having made contact with very compassionate individuals within the Dutch military, the following event took place on August 14, 2015:

Speech by Defence Attaché of the Kingdom of the Netherlands, LtCol Christa Oppers-Beumer, on the occasion of the Mobilization War Cross decoration ceremony in Aylmer, Ontario.

Aylmer, ON, Friday 14 August 2015

NL Defence Attachée's speech in Aylmer, ON

Dear Bebelaar family and guests,

I would like to start this decoration ceremony with the playing of the National Anthem of the Kingdom of the Netherlands.

(playing of "Het Wilhelmus")

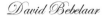

Tomorrow, 15 August, 70 years ago, the Japanese armed forces capitulated, and with that the second World War officially came to an end.

Today, we are here together to award a decoration of honour, posthumously, to Sergeant Jacob Bebelaar and Private Maurits Cornelis Cramer.

They have not been honoured during their lifetime for what they did for the Kingdom of the Netherlands. Unfortunately, they both died as a prisoners of war (POWs), being a sergeant and private in the Royal Netherlands Indies Armed Forces (KNIL).

Sergeant Jacob Bebelaar was a POW at the Siam Birma railroad as of June 1942. He joined the Netherlands Indies Army in December 1941 in Medan and became a POW on 17 March 1942. He fell ill a year later and passed away on 22 June 1943, at the age of 32. At that time his son, Walter (Wouter Jan), was three years old. Jacob has been reburied in a war cemetery in Thanbyuzayat, Myanmar.

Private Maurits Cornelis Cramer joined the Netherlands Indies Army in December 1941 as well. He was also taken POW in March 1942. When he and 1,150 POWs were transported from Palembang, Sumatra to Singapore he died onboard the ship on 28 May 1945 at the age of 40. He was buried at sea. Private Maurits Cornelis Cramer had endured the hardship of POW life for more than 3 years. His son Nicholaas Adrianus Cramer was seven years old when he lost his father.

After the war, life had to go on. Mothers had to raise their children alone and men who returned from the war and the POW camps could not, would not, talk about what they had gone through. Most of their stories stayed untold and their hardship was not recognised. Until today for Sergeant Jacob Bebelaar and Private Maurits Cornelis Cramer.

Due to the voluntary work of Royal Netherlands Military Police officer Marco Huysdens, who was contacted by David Bebelaar in search for recognition for his grandfather, we are able to have this ceremony today in Aylmer. Marco Huysdens has been instrumental in the process of requesting posthumous decorations for David's grandfather and Nick's father. As a result of that, I am here today (as Defence Attache of the Kingdom of the Netherlands representing the Minister of Defence) together with my husband, Peer, to solemnly present the Mobilization War Cross (Mobilisatie Oorlogs Kruis) to Jacob Bebelaar and Maurits Cornelis Cramer.

I would now ask for a moment of silence to pay respect to Jacob Bebelaar and Maurits Cornelis Cramer.

Description of the Mobilization War Cross: The ribbon is purple, which symbolizes mourning, the dark period of war and occupation. Also, there is orange, which symbolizes the loyalty to the Royal Family, the House of Orange.

The medal itself consists of four armed bronze crosses. Also two daggers with the points placed up. There is a helmet placed on top of it, surrounded by a bay leaf wreath that signifies honour.

The helmet and dagger were used by the NL Armed Forces during World War II.

On the back of the medal you can read the inscription: DEN VADERLANT GHETROUWE. This is the second sentence of the NL National Anthemn. It means as much as: "We stand on guard for thee."

Finally, the deserved recognition for someone who gave his life defending the flag of his homeland.

Jacob Bebelaar
May 9, 1911 - June 22, 1943
Captured – March 29, 1942 – Kutacane, Sumatra
Passed – June 22, 1943 – Burma (Three Pagoda Pass)
Sergeant 1st Class in KNIL

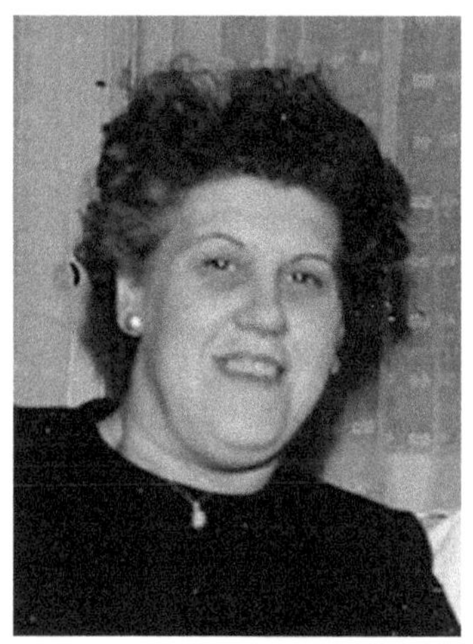

Andrea Pieternella Bebelaar
October 21, 1911 – October 3, 1966
Interned in Sumatra – March 1942 – Brastagi, Aek Pamienke III
Civilian

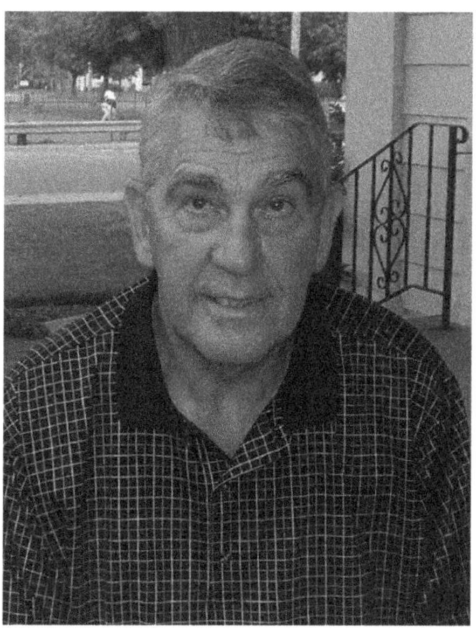

Wouter (Walter) Jan Bebelaar
April 28, 1940 – July 5, 2009
Interned in Sumatra – March 1942 – Brastagi, Aek Pamienke III
Civilian – Child

Acknowledgements

Without the translation services of the following individuals, this compilation would not have been possible: Pol Maenhaut, Tineke Lubbe, Hans Deeg, Paul Michel, and Annamiek/Andre Lankhuijzen. A special thanks also to Marco Huysdens for his tireless efforts to research and lobby for recognition for KNIL soldiers.

CPSIA information can be obtained
at www.ICGtesting.com
Printed in the USA
LVHW080438120119
603662LV00002B/2/P

9 780228 806110